GLADHEARTED
DISCIPLES

GLADHEARTED
DISCIPLES

Equipping Your Congregation *with*
Generous *and* Enduring Faith

Chris Folmsbee

Abingdon Press™

Nashville

GLADHEARTED DISCIPLES:
EQUIPPING YOUR CONGREGATION WITH GENEROUS AND ENDURING FAITH

Copyright © 2015 by Chris Folmsbee

This book is printed on acid-free paper.

Library of Congress Cataloging-in-Publication Data has been requested.

ISBN: 978-1-63088-423-9

Scripture quotations unless noted otherwise are from the Common English Bible. Copyright © 2011 by the Common English Bible. All rights reserved. Used by permission. www.CommonEnglishBible.com.

Scripture quotations marked (KJV) are taken from The Authorized (King James) Version. Rights in the Authorized Version in the United Kingdom are vested in the Crown. Reproduced by permission of the Crown's patentee, Cambridge University Press.

15 16 17 18 19 20 21 22 23 24—10 9 8 7 6 5 4 3 2 1

MANUFACTURED IN THE UNITED STATES OF AMERICA

For Geoff, Brad, and Jeremy

Contents

Part Three
Gladhearted Disciples and Their Embodied Practice

Part Four
Gladhearted Disciples and Their Commitment to Yielded Guidance

Part Five
The Gladhearted Disciple-Making Leader

Acknowledgments

T hanks, Gina, for your help to make this book project a reality. I couldn't have done this without you. Thanks for your friendship, love, and support. Thanks, Megan, Drew, and Luke for believing in me and helping me toward being a more generous and faithful father.

Thanks, Resurrection family, for allowing me the opportunity to serve alongside you as we build a Christian community where nonreligious and nominally religious people are becoming deeply committed Christians.

Thanks, Carol Cartmill, Jane Fowler, Matt Williams, Darrell Holtz, Liz Gyori, Jon Edlin, Phil Antilla, Michelle Funk, and Shari Wilkins for all the conversations in our team meetings that made their way into this book. Thanks, Jeff and Michelle Kirby, for your friendship and support.

Thanks, VIBE community, for allowing me to be one of your pastors. I love worshipping with you each week and look forward to seeing how God continues to shape our community for God's mission. Thanks Wendy Chrostek, James Felver, Jordan Tracy, Cory Ryan, Angela LaVallie, and Tara Houx!

Thank you, Pastor Adam Hamilton, for your vision, leadership, and commitment to the mission of God and The United Methodist Church of the Resurrection. It is a privilege to serve with you.

Introduction: Gladhearted Disciples Defined

When the publishers at Abingdon recommended the title *Glad-hearted Disciples*, I wasn't immediately struck with excitement. In fact, I thought it felt kind of forced and a bit gimmicky. I've written a bunch of books over the last ten years, and this was the first time I hadn't really been jazzed about a title that was presented to me.

My first questions were, "What in the world is a gladhearted disciple? Do I even know one? Can I point one out? Am I a gladhearted disciple?" I struggled a bit to even get my head around how I would describe one let alone write a book for pastors and lay leaders, a book that not only tried to describe a gladhearted disciple but also put forth new ideas and concepts on how to make them.

After several days, however, it grew on me and eventually it hit me. A gladhearted disciple is exactly what I am trying to make. In fact, I am kind of worn out with the pessimism and cynicism that exists among many of the church leaders I run into every now and again. I'm hopeful there will be more reconstructionists who step forward in the days ahead to balance out the necessary, but sometimes overpowering, spirit of deconstruction. It doesn't matter how many pessimists or cynics camouflage their feelings around words like *realist* and *pragmatist*; negative is negative, no matter how you try and explain it away.

Simply said, gladhearted disciples are followers of Jesus who are generous people looking into the future through a lens of hope, accepting but not settling for what the world has become, and yet determined to live in such a way that engages the world in Christ-centered mission, through the empowerment and guidance of the Holy Spirit, and with the purpose of bringing the redemptive reign of God in Christ into every dimension of life. Gladhearted disciples are about one thing—the kingdom of God. The kingdom of God is anywhere God reigns.

Gladhearted disciples are noticeably optimistic people who are pleasant to be around. They are grateful for the work of Jesus on the cross, and it is this atoning work of Jesus that drives them to endure the moments in life that aren't so happy and joyous. They endure in order to find their true self and contentment in the suffering of Jesus. "How can a gladhearted disciple be content in suffering?" I was asked. Here's how; because suffering with Jesus is enduring any and all experiences of hardship for the sake of the gospel, which is ultimately for the sake of the world. We are on our way to being converted into new creatures every day. As gladhearted disciples, we accept this conversion, or suffer with it, so that Christ will be made known or so that ultimately "Thy kingdom come . . . in earth, as it is in heaven" (Matt 6:10 KJV).

The following is a deeper look into what it means to be a gladhearted disciple:

1. **Gladhearted disciples are generous.** A generous life is one that gives without expecting anything in return. A generous person, therefore, is one who loves, knowing full well that there may not be any advantage to or profit from the love. Our churches are filled with generous people, yet we need more of them. This does not mean that occasionally one would give a financial contribution or donate clothing or volunteer in children's Sunday school. These examples are certainly generous acts. However, generous disciples are ones who have mastered their need to think of and act on behalf of themselves first—in all experiences and in all situations. Generous disciples live openhandedly and full of a spirit of grace.

2. **Gladhearted disciples look into the future through a lens of hope.** We will talk more about this in subsequent chapters, so for now I will simply say that hope resides within the follower of Jesus. Hope is a door (Hos 2:15) and it is an "anchor for our whole being" (Heb 6:19) as we await the eventual reality that all things will be made new. Hope is formed through suffering and through ongoing conversion, and it is related to joy, faith, perseverance, and patience. Hope essentially orients and continues to reorient the disciple's life toward what we so desperately and eagerly wait upon but do not yet occupy. In my opinion, hope is the key to the believer living in the present reality, with the capacity to trust that

God is at work, even when it is difficult to spot in the brokenness around us.

3. **Gladhearted disciples live in such a way that engages the world in Christ-centered mission.** I know and have conversations with many Christians who are confused about mission. Somehow they got it into their thinking that discipleship and mission are two entirely separate aspects of faith formation. This could not be further from the truth. While churches often create ministry initiatives that do detach these two areas of practice and divide them from one another, they are not meant to be practices expressed in isolation from one another. Discipleship is for mission. We followers of Jesus are becoming deeply committed Christians because God is a missionary God who sends us into the world to participate with God to restore the world toward its intended wholeness. You don't choose between various discipleship activities and education or mission trips and justice initiatives. Discipleship, or what is increasingly referred to in many churches as *spiritual formation*, is entirely for God's mission. The followers of Jesus engage the world in Christ-centered mission not to "do missions" but to become deeply committed disciples. Mission isn't merely a by-product of discipleship; it is the very reason for discipleship. God sends the Son; the Son sends the Spirit; and the Spirit sends the church to live out the intended ways of God. Gladhearted disciples don't do mission *or* discipleship. Because of mission, gladhearted disciples become authentic, growing agents of God's restoration, and love, in and for the world.

4. **Gladhearted disciples are empowered and guided by the Holy Spirit.** The church is sent and therefore it requires that we are intentional and strategic people. We are not blown by the wind to and fro undecidedly sitting back and waiting for the Holy Spirit to work. However, we do not work on our own. We listen, discern, and act on our church purpose statements because the Spirit leads us—not because we have the authority to do it on our own. Jesus told his disciples in Acts 1 that the Holy Spirit would come upon them and then they would act—doing greater things. The Holy Spirit is what empowers us to actively engage the world for Christ. The Holy Spirit is out in front of us preveniently convicting people, advocating, counseling, comforting, and so on. We don't do the work of the Spirit; we strive to catch up to the Spirit only to

find that the Holy Sprit has gone out ahead of us, once again leading us toward the faithful and effective work of God. Gladhearted
disciples realize that they are empowered and guided by the Holy
Spirit. Gladhearted disciples seek the dynamic ministry of the Holy
Spirit as not only the beginning but also the middle and end of a
faithful commitment to a Christ-centered mission.

5. **Gladhearted disciples know their purpose is to bring the redemptive reign of God in Christ into every dimension of life.** People
who live on mission, or live knowing that discipleship is for God's
mission, do everything they can to live out the kingdom teachings
of Jesus. There are many kingdom teachings of Jesus. None of these
teachings is more pointed than the Beatitudes found in Matthew
5 and Luke 6. For brevity's sake I would encourage you to study
these on your own. However, before you do, don't think of these
Beatitudes as blessings due us when we choose to do them. Instead,
think of the Beatitudes as blessings that God is already doing that
we get to be a part of. We aren't blessed when we are perform-
ing the Beatitudes. We are blessed because we get to live them out
with and in the presence of God. Below is a short synopsis of the
Beatitudes or the kingdom virtues from Matthew 5. These ways
of engagement are specific things we can do to live in and live out
the kingdom of God every day. Remember, these are not duties of
gladhearted disciples; these are practices of joyful participation in
which we participate in God's redemptive purposes. We participate
with God when we:

- 5:3—are humble before God, identifying with the humble—
  the poor, the social outcasts

- 5:4—mourn or grieve with sincere repentance toward God
  and then find ways to comfort others who mourn

- 5:5—are surrendered to God, committing ourselves to finding and following God toward peace and making peace

- 5:6—hunger and thirst for delivering justice that brings
  people into community with God, self, others, and the world

- 5:7—practice mercy through compassionate acts and faithful
  generosity toward any and all in need

- 5:8—seek God's will of peace with life-encompassing integrity

- 5:9—find ways to make peace with all enemies, as God shows life to God's enemies

- 5:10-12—are willing to suffer as Jesus did, because of our loyalty to Jesus and his teachings about making right what is wrong in the world.[1]

So this is our calling: to make disciples, gladhearted ones at that. While Jesus didn't say to make gladhearted disciples in Matthew 28, the Great Commission, I think implicit within Jesus's teaching was a desire for all of his followers to be gladhearted. To move us forward to a deeper understanding of what it means to be a gladhearted disciple, I remind you of my definition of a gladhearted disciple: Gladhearted disciples are followers of Jesus who are generous people looking into the future through a lens of hope, accepting but not settling for what the world has become and yet determined to live in such a way that engages the world in Christ-centered mission, through the empowerment and guidance of the Holy Spirit, and with the purpose of bringing the redemptive reign of God in Christ into every dimension of life.

How to Use This Book

I have designed this book with the intention that you may use it in a variety of ways and in multiple settings. My goal, of course, is that this book would inspire you to go beyond personal study and reflection and that you would be compelled to use it with staff leadership teams, volunteer leadership teams, small groups, various classes, and entire congregations. Nothing would please me more than to know that this book is:

- **Providing a way for you and your congregation to be encouraged, challenged, and equipped.** Sometimes congregations and the leadership of these congregations can feel stuck. Congregations can feel like they need something more or that something is missing or keeping them from moving past their current methods of programming and discipleship. This book can help you discover new ways and new reasons for doing what you do, ultimately leading you into more effective ways of congregational discipleship.

- **Providing several weeks of curriculum for your groups or classes.** Small groups and classes are always looking for fresh curriculum to engage the group in new and challenging ways. This book can be used to deepen each person's understanding of what it means to become a deeply committed Christian.

- **Providing a teaching or preaching outline.** This book has been designed in such a way that it could be used as a template for a discipleship class or a preaching outline. The five parts of this book could easily be used to craft a five-week class or preaching series.

- **Providing a way to bring your teams together for deeper thought and broader action.** Paid staff teams and lay or volunteer staff teams could benefit from the ideas and practical tools in this book. This book will also help teams of all kinds evaluate their effectiveness, help them wrestle with tough questions and ideas, and challenge them to discover innovative ways to call people to follow in the footsteps of Jesus.

- **Providing college and seminary students with fodder for conversation and practice.** This book will challenge the norms of discipleship, and it can be used in a myriad of ways to engage the thinking of emerging leaders: shaping within them practices for their current or future ministry context.

At the end of the book you will find questions from each chapter. These questions are meant for reflection and discussion. These questions can be used in each of the settings listed above and probably many more teaching and learning contexts. These questions are meant to help each person dig deeper into the ideas of this book through conversation, study, or reflection.

Part One

MAKING DISCIPLES:
A NEW APOLOGETIC

Chapter 1

A New Apologetic for a Post-Christian World

The modern era was a time when rational arguments and logical reasoning was the primary way of convincing nonreligious people to turn to Jesus. Those days are gone and those methods of helping nonreligious people find and follow Jesus are dead. In the place of those methods is a new apologetic characterized by human aesthetics, imaginative expression, and inspired living.

This new apologetic makes more innate sense to the faithfully skeptical than the circular arguments and facts about Christianity that they have come to justifiably scrutinize. This scrutiny is largely based on the observations they make about Christians not the facts about Christianity. For the church to most faithfully engage today's skeptic, it must move away from an apologetic based primarily on reason and logic and inspire people toward exploring God through the recognition and participation in the story of God.

This new apologetic is interesting to skeptics and explorers of the Christian. This new apologetic heightens the senses of everyday people in everyday life, legitimizing the gospel and kingdom life for all who see, touch, hear, taste, and smell it. Gladhearted disciple making is the new apologetic. We need to embrace it, or the gospel story will remain nothing more than something for skeptics and explorers to scoff at, disparage, and explicitly dismiss. The Christian church is God's promise and God's plan to serve the world. Gladhearted disciples, therefore, are to be the agents of such an apologetic. The sanctifying church must become the kingdom society that helps its current and future adherents turn innate missional instincts into outward missional expressions and embodiment.

Where Missional Instincts Come From

Missional instincts are found within each one of us. God fearer or not, the native impulse to help someone who is in need (whether acted upon or not), to smile at the sight of two people in love, to weep with another in a time of remembrance or loss, and to shout for joy alongside another in a moment of celebration unequivocally comes from the missional instincts born into the heart, mind, and soul of all of humanity. We are heirs of the examples above as well as a host of other emotional, spiritual, intellectual, physical, and social native impulses. Each one of us has been created in the image of God. Missional instincts come from within wholly because they were breathed into each one of us when God chose to imaginatively and outwardly express what was a native impulse from within. It was the native impulse of God that birthed humanity and creation.

To be created in the image of God simply means that we bear something of God's likeness—God's nature, splendor, wisdom, and morality. We resemble God. Therefore, we are God's promised and planned medium in which to deliver the enduring message of peace (salvation) and justice that works itself out through hope and healing to the shattered world around us.

We best comprehend and actualize the image of God through three key lines of thought—natural, political, and moral.[1] Each of these three concepts uniquely provides a divergent angle in which to explore accurately what it means to have been created in the image of God and to live into that actuality.

We've been created with spirit, just as God is spirit. Unlike God (the Father), however, we have also been created with flesh in which to hospitably accommodate our spirits. John Wesley once alluded to the idea that God did not create humanity as merely matter and out of a meaningless, unintelligent clump of mud, but as a spirit just like God.[2] We've been created in the natural likeness of God. We have missional instincts because we share the natural likeness of God.

This natural likeness means that in our spirits we've been created with the wisdom and understanding that allows us to know evil from good, the desire or will to do the good we know, and the absolute freedom to choose between a life that follows God or an anthropocentric life characterized by self-satisfaction, narcissism, and a host of other indulgent and ignorant traits.

Along with being created in the natural likeness of God, we've also been created in the political likeness of God. Humanity is not only in relationship with one another but also in relationship with the entirety of the created world.

We've been formed to participate with God in caring for humanity and for the natural world. We have missional instincts because we share the political likeness of God.

We've also been designed in the moral likeness of God. We've been decidedly and distinctly created to worship God with truth and the righteousness of our lives in order that we might reflect the holiness of God. We have faithful instincts because we share the moral likeness of God.

The natural, political, and moral likeness in which we've been formed and are being formed is precisely where the innate desire to live faithfully is born and takes up residence. With that said, it is imperative for gladhearted disciples to help nonreligious people notice God's likeness within them; it really isn't about how far skeptics are from God but rather just how closely they've been created to resemble God. This truth begins to shape a new way of apologetics. It isn't reason, and it isn't truth as told by us that captures the heart of the nonreligious person. It is, instead, the connection to the missional instincts or native impulses that helps close the believability gap—the space between dogma and everyday religion where we find Jesus-centered mission.

Hence, the desire to do right, to live wholly, to be about the things of God takes residence within each one of us. It is this inner disposition and our posture that guide us toward becoming people of intentional mission. Likewise, it is expressly the instinctual mission that guides gladhearted disciples to live out God's story through missional expressions of hope and healing.

What Missional Instincts Involve and Imply

To be missional, gladhearted disciples is to participate in God's redemptive work of restoring the world toward its intended wholeness. Missional living is a participatory life that is without center or circumference. There is no specific geographical or other position that holds us near or keeps us from afar. People of mission, of generous and enduring living, are unambiguous about joining in the activity of God in every possible place, be it urban, suburban, rural, and so on.

As gladhearted disciples we are people who:

- Consider ourselves missionaries who are always looking for ways to contextualize the gospel story[3]

- Learn about others through intentional listening as opposed to calculated arguments

- Practice forbearance towards those who don't believe as we do

- Celebrate the multicultural composition of God's kingdom

- Seek to be formed through an ongoing commitment to spiritual practices such as prayer, fasting, study, simplicity, and so on

- Ask and allow others to ask questions about God without offense

- Connect ourselves with sociological concerns and implications

- Care for God's creation through efforts to live environmentally conscious

- Trust in the conversation consisting of self, others, *and* the Holy Spirit

- Are comfortable with doubt as a key ingredient in faith formation—both in self and in others

- Are keenly aware of social injustices in a local, regional, and global context

- Use the imagination to evoke inspiration and welcome illumination

- Value the unique personalities and idiosyncrasies of others and seek to build healthy relationships with them

- Embrace and endorse the mystery of God, realizing that God's work is neither predictable nor conventional

- Believe that the church is the anointed and appointed earthly body of Christ sanctified to be the primary agent of God's restoration

- Inspire others through a life of generosity and hospitality

- Find deep meaning in both the context and meaning of Jesus's birth, life, death, resurrection, and ascension

Involvement with God's mission has implications. Some implications are unique to us based on our own circumstances, occasions, and events of life. Other implications, however, we share with all other Christians throughout the earth.

Missional instincts direct our life. Out of these missional instincts gladhearted disciples re-narrate meaning, purpose, and hope, causing us to live into a new story. These instincts are not to remain internal. Ultimately we are to allow the Holy Spirit to take the instincts within each of us and turn them into missional expressions—evidence of a life as God designed it to be.

What Missional Expressions Reveal

If the image of God, in which we were unquestionably created, is the impetus for the missional instincts found within gladhearted disciples, then the action taken because of those instincts is the energy for the missional expressions that we choose to live out. These expressions are precisely how we resemble God or live into the image in which we were so thoughtfully and wonderfully created.

When missional instincts move to become missional expressions, the nature, splendor, wisdom, and ethics of God are exposed to the world. In a sense, humanity opens the elements of God's nature to the world, profoundly revealing the missional heart of God. God's heart is filled with an assortment of forms of divine consideration toward creation. God's considerations for all of creation are simple. God's missionary heart reveals an intention to restore the world toward the wholeness in which it was designed. The anthem of God's distinction is one of salvation and justice to a world otherwise left shattered and hopeless. We are the express image of God so that the world would be made good, right, or better still, beautifully whole. Gladhearted disciples are the image of God so that the world we come into contact with might know, above all else, that God has not forgotten them.

Every moment of our participation in God's mission to restore the world is a declaration from God. Every kind word, every dollar given, every hand held, every meal served, every gospel story shared, every house repaired, every thirsty mouth quenched, every wound bandaged, every blanket meant for warmth, every shout of joy or tear of sorrow shared with another, every hospital bedside visit, every smile meant to brighten the day of another, and so on and so on is a missional expression declaring to the world, God has not forgotten you. In that declaration the world finds hope, healing, and eventually heavenly peace or shalom. Not the kind of peace that we think of in opposition to war (although I hope that to be the case too) but rather the kind of peace that arrives out of union with God, harmony with self, community with others, and delight in all of creation.

Gladhearted disciples are beautiful. When I refer to *beauty*, I am not speaking merely of the kind that is emotional or mystical. I am talking about the kind of beauty that is seen through our eyes or felt throughout the depths of our heart and soul. Although the kind of beauty that one might find in another human, the beauty from a mountain vista, or the beauty found in canvases hanging on the wall of a gallery are certainly genuine and significant, I am referring to a beauty that can be found among the most impoverished areas of a city, in the utter lack of loveliness in another or the complete darkness of divorce or the pain of a memorial service or funeral. I am referring to a beauty that endures regardless of how undiscovered or unnoticed or absent it might be or appear to be. I am referring to a beauty that is quite simply the ultimate dialect of God, love.

The sacredness of the gladhearted disciples' existence is not the life we live—it is the love we live. It is out of love that life is generously and enduringly lived. A beautiful life is not one measured only by splendor, attractiveness, or excellence. Love almost single-handedly measures the essence of beauty. In the midst of the worst or the best, God is love. Love exists because God exists. Love is felt because God is present. Where God is present, God is fully there—not giving a bit of God's love, but giving all of God's love. God speaks love, and love takes the abstraction out of truth and puts the concrete in it. We know God is truth because God is personal.[4] Gladhearted disciples know God personally and have ongoing encounters with the personality of God.

I am fully aware that there are many places in this world where love is not articulated, displayed, or felt. One of the people in my small group shared with the rest of us that she is "100 percent sure" that her dad doesn't love her. I don't know if that is true or not, but I do know there are many, many places where love is evidently absent. That doesn't mean, however, that God is not love or that God is not present. It simply means that humanity is not acting on its most basic natural impulse or missional instinct, love.

Nothing is beautiful without love. Even matters outside the realm of humanity, but within the realm of creation, such as a painting, a song, a sculpture, a flower, or an animal, are not without love. God is love and God is everywhere and, therefore, in everything that is beautiful there is God and God's love. Gladhearted disciples are driven by God's loving presence.

Missional expressions of gladhearted disciples are born out of the missional instincts gifted to us through the image in which we have been created. Missional expressions declare that God has not forgotten us, and that salvation and justice provide the hope, healing, and peace necessary for a world to be made good, right, and ultimately whole—to be made just the way that God intended it to be.

Missional expressions reveal that God is love and that love is indeed what measures the essence of beauty. A theology of love, as applied by the glad-hearted disciples' life, is the footing for a new apologetic.

The Death, Burial, and Nonresurrection of Modern Apologetics

I am not implying that love was not the foundation or at least the intended foundation for modern apologetics. Nevertheless, one of the fundamental differences between the new apologetic (missional living) and apologetics of yesteryear is not exclusive to how one postures oneself to resemble God but is rather the posture of the ones on the other end of the resembling. For the skeptical, whether seeking or not, the posture may very well be one of inquisition and analysis. However, there is a very good chance that the queries of the nonreligious are not inherent in apologetics that most of Christianity has been equipped to give. Is it not possible that the nonreligious don't care about our "truth"? Is it even more possible that the nonreligious may have a question that we can't answer, making our series of anecdotal apologetics irrelevant?

I can't remember the last time that I had a conversation with one of my next-door neighbors, friends, family members, or complete strangers that began with the evidences of the divine inspiration of the Bible, the fulfilled prophecies, the unique historical accuracies, the unique structure, the scientific accuracies, or archeological findings that support the Bible. At least, I haven't had conversations with the before mentioned at the beginning of their inquisition or even in the center of their disbelief and uncertainty. Many of the apologetic triumphs previously employed to convince nonreligious people to turn to Jesus are not remotely relevant to the nonreligious person's life or pertinent to the questions they are asking.

What I can vividly remember from conversations with everyday people about God, faith, and life, however, are matters related to everyday living. They are matters related to the person who shot and killed a doctor who performs abortions or the conduct of priests and church leaders (don't merely think Catholicism here) toward little boys and girls or massive oil spills that are killing entire ecosystems. Other common questions revolve around the inability of most Christians to carry on a conversation about faith or religions of another kind without it turning into an argument, trial, or at the very least, a "blame storming" exercise. In fact, in a conversation with one of my neighbors regarding the church, he said, "Nothing beautiful can come out of the church." Therein lies the impetus for this book. I believe the church filled with gladhearted disciples is the very society called to missional living, and the key to missional living is the making of gladhearted disciples.

There was a day when modern apologetics were helpful. That day is no more. Rationalizing God, faith, and life through logical lines of reasoning for the purpose of a systematic account of all things Christian and to expose the flaws of other worldviews leaves modern apologists looking absurdly unaware and boorish. Gladhearted disciples know that their life is the most helpful apologetic for today's post-Christian culture.

It is incredibly naïve to have an issue with apologetics as a system of definition and organized evidences, or with specific apologists for that matter. The Apostle Paul, Tertullian, Justin Martyr, Augustine, Thomas Aquinas, and C. S. Lewis, to name a few Christian apologists, were all amazing people doing amazing work. We have all learned a lot from the writing of these people and have learned even more from those who have learned from these men. The modern apologist has paved the way for the rest of us. In spite of this, the answer we are to give to "anyone [who] asks you to speak of your hope"[5] must be directly related to the questions people are asking, not the answers we wish to give. The questions being asked today are different from the questions that must have been asked in previous generations. That's the only reason I can think that modern apologetics must have been at one time relevant—because the questions being asked determined them.

Not one of us could confess to know the questions that were being asked thirty, forty, fifty, one hundred, or two hundred years ago, or the attitude in which they were being asked. However, I do, like you, have hundreds of books and thousands of websites at my fingertips, and these resources lead me to believe that if love was the motive or intended footing of modern apologetics then the answers that many of us have been trained to give must have been directly connected to the questions being asked at the individual times they were asked. I conclude, therefore, that since the answers I have been trained over the years to give no longer are relevant answers to the questions that I am being asked, then the questions being asked today must be different than those in the modern era.

But straightforward logic isn't what is needed. What is needed is an apologetic based on love and driven by aesthetics, imaginative expression, and inspired living. What is principally needed is a gladhearted apologetic centered on missional living that heightens the senses of everyday people in everyday life, legitimizing the gospel and kingdom life for all who see, touch, hear, taste, and smell it.

One more note on this: I am sure that there are many people alive today with a modern mind-set. These people may very well be in need of a more rationalistic and logical line of reasoning to help them make sense of the Christian faith. This, however, is not the future. The number of post-Christian people living in this post-Christian world is only increasing. Don't believe me? Ask the teachers of the third, fourth, and fifth graders of your local elementary school if the approach to life is changing. For many of you reading this book, the approach to life has already completely changed.

This is why we must shift the modernistic Christian apologetic training and equipping of emerging adults and children a new way. We must find a way to move ourselves beyond what we know and admit that there are things about our culture that we don't even know we don't know.

A movement away from modern apologetics doesn't take away the importance of the data or the information or even the experiences that have been collected over time about the Christian faith. The fulfilled prophecies, historical accuracies, biblical uniquenesses, and so on are important. However, they are more helpful to a person who has already encountered God and decided to choose Jesus as the director of his or her life than they are to a person who is wondering about the sheer relevance of Christianity. We should teach our emerging adults and children what we have learned through the modern era; we just shouldn't be starting there if the faithfully skeptical and distrustfully curious aren't starting there and frankly, I think they aren't.

We need to bury modern apologetics (or at the very least collectively admit that the need for modern apologetics is rapidly declining) in favor of an apologetic that evokes the imagination and paints a living rendering of the way God intended life and the world to be—beautiful. We bury old technologies, educational methods, medical practices, business strategies, and so on every day in favor of what works and feels better for our current context. I know that authors aren't supposed to ask too many "one-way" questions in the body of their work but I just have to ask: Why are we so afraid to move away from modern apologetics? Are we really losing anything? Or are we, in fact, gaining a whole lot more?

So much of the Christian faith (especially evangelicalism) is regulated by fear. What are we so afraid of? Does the God who reigns today not have as much of the world in control as we once knew and trusted? Is the Holy Spirit not as much of a guide as we once knew? Do we somehow believe that if we move away from a modern approach to apologetics that we will no longer have anything to say? Instead, will we have to become something different and turn over control of our missional instincts and expressions to a God who we know moves mysteriously? Honestly, why are we so fearful? Consider this assertion from Joseph Gremillion: "The 'Church' and the 'world' are not identical, but neither are they in irrevocable opposition. For, while the 'Church' transcends the 'world,' it also exists *in* the world. Existing there, it has an assignment to seek to transform the world according to the mind of and message of Christ."[6] Don't we wish to find the most relevant approach to apologetics in order that we might be able to do our "duty" as outlined above? Surely, for the sake of the world, we desire to discover a new way of apologetics.

The Nature of Faithful Expressions

The mission of God is to restore the world toward its intended wholeness. God is actively using the kingdom society, the church, filled with gladhearted disciples, to carry out this mission. When the church participates in God's mission it paints a living rendering of the way that God intended life and the world to be—beautiful and completely whole.

The mission is God's. It is not a movement of the church but an attribute of God that involves the Son and the Spirit through the Father that includes the church. The church, therefore, does not manufacture mission; it simply yields to the Spirit as it carries out the work of the mission that Jesus came to model.

The nature of God's mission is composed of three indivisible aspects—scripture, culture, and our faith communities. A missional apologetic, consequently, must take into account these three aspects of God's mission as it deconstructs models of apologetics that no longer work and reconstructs an effective model for today. As the church seeks to find genuine ways to integrate scripture, culture making, and the practices of our faith community into its daily rhythms, it begins to assemble an apologetic built squarely on the mission of God as viewed through the lens of the entire gospel story. This full narrative view of the story and mission of God is what drives missional disciples to integrate scripture into everything they do, to seek to understand the cultural context of the world around them, and to intentionally foster the growth of their faith communities.

The Progress of Missional Expressions

Missional expressions manifest themselves in a variety of ways. Each of these expressions is essential to the construction of a new kind of apologetic—a third way—a way of living beautifully. Without these expressions we might remain convinced that one of the two other ways of apologetics is no longer valid, but I fear that we'll just sit around on our hands wondering what we should do next. These expressions are intentional patterns of beautiful living that reveal God and God's intended ways of life to a broken world.

The three missional expressions to integrate into your everyday life are holiness (both personal and communal), embodied practice, and yielded guidance. By *holiness* I mean the frequency and duration of the holy moments in our life. By *embodied practice* I mean the intentional ways we choose to participate in God's mission to restore the world toward its intended wholeness. Finally, by *yielded guidance* I expressly mean our desire and commitment to allow the Holy Spirit to direct our lives. We'll cover each of these in greater detail in the pages to follow.

Chapter 2

What a New Apologetic Looks Like in a Post-Christian World

I can't remember the first time I heard the term *post-Christian*, but I am sure that I was insulted or at the very least unnerved. How could anyone, especially those in the church, deem the world to be post-Christian? I think I was listening to my friend Brian McLaren teach at a conference I was attending when I first heard it. If that was the first time, it completely jolted me and left me shaking my head. I have never liked it.

Honestly, the term suggests something that I do not want to admit. The term suggests that Christianity is in decline and that it no longer occupies a central position in culture. A post-Christian culture simply means that we are moving toward complete secularization of the world. We are increasingly moving toward a post-Christian culture where Christianity is not the primary worldview when it comes to politics, education, religion, or any other societal or personal value. Because Christianity is not the primary worldview, it means that to most people (especially Millennials and the currently named Generation Z to follow) concepts from the Bible may be not only unfamiliar but also completely alien. Most of the Millennials who I have spiritual conversations with have many questions about life and faith. These questions are not, however, questions of the inerrancy of scripture or the historicity of Jesus. The questions are usually more about the evil that is found in such injustices as widespread genocide, human trafficking, global poverty, and so on. I've had fewer than a dozen Millennials who are exploring God ask me about the accuracy or validity of the Bible. In contrast, hundreds ask me why there is suffering, disease, and tragedy.

The use of the term *post-Christian* used to scare me and make me want to stand on the rooftops shouting at the top of my lungs that the world was going to hell in a handbasket. Today, however, this term doesn't scare me at all. In fact, it makes me energized about the opportunity that the church has to realize its full potential and move from a place of irrelevance to a place of remarkable importance. To move toward a place of relevance, however, the church must change its perspective and practice of apologetics. Apologetics can no longer base its arguments for the Christian faith on a book that most of the world doesn't even find any sense of credibility within, except as an amazing literary masterpiece. For far too long we have said, "Well, the Bible says . . ." The world around us doesn't care what the Bible says; it cares what our actions say. The Bible is no longer what we thought it was. It is not the standard for life. It may remain the bestselling book of all time but it is no longer the end-all book on how to develop, maintain, and sustain an honorable life. I believe it can be and should be, but isn't.

A few weeks ago I was having dinner out with my wife. One of the servers who came to the table recognized me from church and said, "Do you work at a church near here?"

I replied, "Yes, I do. Do you attend a church near here?"

His response? "No way. I just went to an event one night on sacred art and architecture because my former professor was presenting on Bach."

"Why 'no way'?" I asked.

"Because there is no way I am going to church. I am not sure they would let me in. I'm gay, and the church I went to when I was a kid taught that gay people aren't allowed into heaven. And if I am not allowed into heaven, why should I go to church?"

"That's a great point," I said. "What makes you think that gay people don't get into heaven?"

He responded with, "They [the church he grew up in] said the Bible said so."

"What if I told you that I didn't believe that and that the way I read the Bible leaves room for a whole lot of people to get into heaven—even gay people?"

"That would be great," he said. "But I can't believe that because the people I know who believe in the Bible are just small-minded and arrogant."

The issue for this young man was not merely about being gay and whether gay people "make it into heaven." The issue for this young man was that the people who he knows who "believe" the Bible to be true act small-mindedly and arrogantly. This has to change. Millennials are not concerned about the validity of the Bible as much as they are concerned about people being nice, open-minded, and humble. I am not trying to make a statement on the gay issue here (although I have some thoughts on this too). Don't get lost in your own belief or opinions around the issue here. Many young people won't go to church because of what they think they know about Christians. And we wonder why our world is becoming post-Christian?

Churches, the answer is not to hire younger, cooler-looking staff and build edgier programs. The answer is to give Millennials a larger framework for God and to push their boundaries of God, thus changing their concept of God. Far too often I hear from churches that they are starting a program to reach nonreligious young people. I'm thrilled to find the passion and sometimes blown away by the carefully planned-out methods. However, in the end, the programs and methods typically fall short because Millennials are not looking for programs and methods to connect with God and others. They can do this anytime they want, wherever they want, whenever they want. Millennials are not looking for us to provide a room for them to meet in and have some snacks. Millennials are looking for meaning in their vocation, opportunities to work in partnership for the greater good, amusement and adventure, and the openness to choose what *they* want to talk about and what questions *they* want to ask. Sometimes the worst thing we can do is program for what we think others want. Instead, remembering it is a post-Christian culture, we should be looking for ways to spark younger people's imaginations, fuel their passions and dreams, and offer them a chance to contribute to God's mission to restore the world regardless of their beliefs and convictions, and individualized to their multiple ways of self-expression. This will broaden their concept of God and their perception of the church.

What Millennials, and the generations to follow, need from the church and gladhearted disciples are meaningful conversations, dependable relationships, faithful leadership and mentoring, a commitment to missional discipleship, and a lasting promise of enduring inclusivity. More than all of these, for Millennials, however, is a big concept of God. The smaller we make God seem, the less likely Millennials are going to engage with the church. Each of these significant desires within the hearts and minds of Millennials must be enveloped by ruthless truth-telling, hope, compassion, nontraditional thinking, diversity, complexity, beauty, deep-rooted values, and practical solutions to common problems.

Within walking distance of our church are a few good restaurants that are ideal spots for enjoying a good meal after Bible study. A group of volunteers and I gathered at one restaurant for several weeks in a row because it was close, had good food and service, and on certain nights had cheap beverages. One night the server asked one of my friends, "You guys live around here?"

"Not far. But we work together every Tuesday night at Resurrection," my friend responded.

"What's Resurrection?" the server asked.

Another one of our friends replied, "It is a church."

"Oh. The one right across the parking lot?"

"Yes," I said. "Have you ever been there?"

"Nah. I don't usually get along with church people," he said.

"Why is that?" someone from our table asked.

His response: "Because I have too many big questions and their answers are always too small and packaged."

This person was looking for the church to admit that sometimes things are too hard for easy answers. This person would rather have the church admit that some things are just too complicated to really have a nice and neatly packaged answer. This is one of the major challenges facing gladhearted disciples living in a post-Christian culture. Many Christians have wrestled with the Bible and the somewhat-unanswerable questions of life and have either learned to live without knowing an answer, live in the tension of multiple answers, or come to an answer that may seem clear to them but far-fetched to a young person who didn't grow up getting ready for church as a kid. For many, especially Millennials, the best response is not to quickly answer their question with certainty and dogma. Rather, for many, the best response to a difficult question of life, such as why good people have bad things happen to them, is not a well-thought-out and immediate thesis but an acknowledgement that life is difficult and sometimes there is no painless answer or response.

This is a post-Christian world. It is not churched and it is not primarily viewed as Christian. For some, this is devastating and a reason to panic and live in fear. For others, like gladhearted disciples, it is a blessing in disguise because it allows for what searching Millennials want—conversation, relationship, leadership, missional causes in which to collaborate, and inclusivity that loves without reason. The old, modern apologetics that "rationally" argued to prove prophetic fulfillment, the existence of God before time, and the preeminence of Christianity over other religions are not what the church needs to be relevant and impactful now. No, instead, we need an apologetic that is rooted in the purest aspect of the gospel, love. That isn't to say that the modern apologetic framework doesn't have a place in the conversation. But it doesn't have a place being first in the conversations with nonreligious people, especially Millennials.

Gladhearted disciples recognize that the church is no longer the epicenter of social village life and hasn't been for a long time. Gladhearted disciples, instead, take their faith into the public spaces of village life. Through their commitment to love God and love others, they don't seek to first prove anything except their desire for meaningful conversations, dependable relationships, faithful leadership and mentoring, a commitment to missional discipleship, and a lasting promise of enduring inclusivity.

Part Two

GLADHEARTED DISCIPLES AND THEIR WAYS OF HOLINESS

Chapter 3

Taking Up Residence
with God

Nearly every week I help lead one of the services at our church. The service takes place in our student center; however, a wide variety of ages attend. We've got kids playing with toys in the back and people well into their late seventies worshipping all in one space. It is absolutely beautiful. We say that Vibe is "modern worship for all ages" and to this point, it's a very real way to describe the community that gathers each week. The music is modern. The community worships passionately and very nearly all ages are represented.

After offering the pastoral prayer one Sunday a twenty-something came up to me after the service and said, "Chris, I loved your prayer. Thank you so much. One question, however. What does it mean to take up residence with God? You prayed that we would 'take up residence with God' in your prayer, and honestly I have never heard that phrase before. Could you explain what this means?" So I took about ten or fifteen minutes to share with this person that to take up residence with God simply means that we intentionally choose to find consistent ways to settle in and dwell with God. To dwell with God means that we seek to discover expressive and consistent ways to inhabit the spaces where God is residing—or said differently, to discover areas of our communities or pockets of time where God is redeeming creation to wholeness, to peace.

I continued to explain what I meant by taking up residence with God and that the word *abide* comes from the word *abode*, and when we desire to live into and therefore manifest the intended ways of God we choose to pursue the matters of importance to God—God's sacred rhythms. We search for the fullness in which we were created. This means that we work to live in complete harmony with God, self, others, and the entire cosmos.

"God's sacred rhythms?" she asked.

I said, "You know grace, mercy, truth, life, love, and peace—all of the radiant and majestic things that make God who God is."

"Wow," she said. "That seems really hard. Where do I start?"

Great question, yes? Where do we begin when we are seeking to live into the intended ways of God? Where do we begin when we are seeking to find where God is expressing God's unsurpassed love—redeeming something we might ordinarily consider irredeemable? Where do we help point our congregations onto the on ramp of taking up residence with God?

One of the first and best ways we must help our congregations to take up residence with God is simply to see the world as God sees the world. How does God see the world? God sees the world through a lens of grief or sorrow, anguish and woe. God's heart aches for this world to be made right—the way that God intended it to be. The brokenness that surrounds all of us pains God and, to take up residence with God, it must pain us also. When our heart aches as it fills with sorrow for the broken world around us, we begin to know what it means to see the world as God sees it. This is not to mean that God only sees the world through moments of anguish, sorrow, and misery. God sees the celebrations of this world and celebrates with us too, no doubt. However, it is clear from even a cursory reading of the biblical narrative that God desires the world to be made as it was created to be—whole—and where it isn't, it is breaking God's heart.

Grief often leads us toward action filled with generous love that gives a name and a face to authentic compassion. When our hearts hurt for the pain around us, it leads us toward a faithful stream of unremitting social action and service. God lives where there is brokenness too. God does not merely reside in the hallways of our all-too put-together stain-glassed, polished churches, where we often mask the true condition of our soul. God lives with the family experiencing divorce. God lives with the men and women diagnosed with cancer. God lives with the prisoners who lie awake every night remembering their wrong actions and crying out to someone, anyone, who will listen, all the while wishing they could have back that moment in time. God lives with the alcoholic who can't stop his open hand from smacking the face of his child. God lives with the prostitute who keeps saying, "This is the last time." God is absolutely present in the ugly, the gross, the rage-filled, the bloody, and the filthy. The question is, Are we residing there also? Are we, as gladhearted disciples, pointing our congregations toward joining God? Do we believe that God redeems where there seems to be no hope? Taking up residence with God means that we see the brokenness of this world and we are gutted—we have that sick-to-our-stomach feeling that reminds us, this is not what God intended. Then, gutted to the core, we act. We act swiftly and generously, doing whatever it takes to reverse the tragic trends of a misguided and mistaken world. This is what it means, in part, to take up residence with God.

Some view the world through a lens of disgust. Viewing the world through a lens of disgust can and often does lead to hatred. When hatred emerges out of the disgust, it is usually surrounded by distrust, thinking the worst of humanity, and a pessimism that forces our heart to beat with panic and angst rather than peace and hope. Let me illustrate this for you.

A gentlemen stopped me in the parking lot after a class I had just finished teaching on the kingdom of God. As we stood under the lights with bugs swarming our heads he said, "Did you see the news tonight?"

"No, I haven't seen the news yet. I'll probably check when I get home," I said.

"Probably a good thing you haven't seen it yet," he stated. "There is a story about a mom who fell asleep without putting her kids to bed. They found her five-year-old daughter like a mile down the road all by herself with nothing but her underwear on. Can you believe it? They ought to lock that mom for good! People like that have no business raising kids!"

"You don't really believe that, do you—that they ought to lock that mom up for good?" I said. "We don't know all of the circumstances surrounding that situation. It was dangerous for sure but I am sure that the mom didn't mean to allow for this to happen and she's probably overwhelmed and feeling alone."

"I sure hope she is devastated! Maybe it'll teach her a lesson! All of those people are that way!" he exclaimed, as he walked to his car clearly ready for the conversation to be done.

I, too, walked to my car, opened the door, hopped inside, started it up, and sat there for a minute. My first thought was, "Wow, I must not have done a very good job teaching about the kingdom of God tonight! He did not get it!" My second thought was, "What was that? Surely he doesn't think that *all* people in the urban areas have a propensity to just leave their kids alone in the middle of the night to wander the streets." I sat there for a minute trying to get myself together, said a prayer for the mom of this child and a prayer for the child, and drove home.

Disgust led this person to believe things that just aren't real—what some might describe as thoughts of hate. Disgusted with the news story, likely frustrated with the brokenness of the world, and quite possibly dealing with some personal issues of his own, this man's heart was crammed with disgust. This man, not even knowing the mom or child, let disgust get the best of his heart and grip it tightly. Disgust was gripping this man's heart so tightly it was causing him to make statements that were not only ridiculous but also certainly not gladhearted. This man was repulsed by the fact that someone could allow something like this to happen to his or her child. Instead of grieving for the situation and being concerned for the mom and child, his condition led him to a far-too-often-lived-out snobbery and privilege that somehow makes him (like so many others) feel like he is better than everyone else because he would never allow such a thing to happen. I don't know this man's name or anything about him. I haven't seen him again since that summer night. If he had kids, I am sure he wasn't perfect. Maybe the police didn't find one of his kids a mile from his house alone in the middle of the night wearing nothing but underwear; as a parent, however, I can promise you he wasn't and isn't fault-free. My heart hurts and aches for people who are so full of disgust it makes them think and say hateful things. The scary part is, this is just one end of a spectrum—the end that seems somewhat tame considering the hatred that exists in our broken, yet redeemable world.

No one likes a broken world. No one that I know gets a kick out of seeing people flounder in pain and suffering. Sure, we could name people who have done gruesome things to people throughout history and claimed to have enjoyed it. The kind of people who do such things, however, are not in a healthy state of mind, body, and spirit. No one likes war, disease, tragedy, infidelity, addiction, death, and all of the many things that make this world broken—but such is the world in which we live, and God chose to reside in this world in the person of Jesus. Gladhearted disciples accept the way the world is but expectantly wait for God's redemptive activity.

To take up residence with God, therefore, involves first and foremost viewing the world through a lens of grief, rather than disgust, realizing that we are God's holy arm, the people of God chosen to take action and live out the intended ways of God. The people of God are chosen to "unbreak" the world. It is through this way of life that gladhearted disciples practice resurrection, manifest hope, and mediate God's presence to a hurting world, seeking to genuinely and openhandedly practice a witness marked by enduring love for all those in need.

Chapter 4

The Organization and Essence of Community

Want to see a puzzled look? Ask the congregants in your church what community is—ask them to define the term *community*. You'll get a slew of answers, all of which are probably characteristics implicit within a community. It is likely, however, you won't hear a definition descriptive enough to truly explain community.

The word *community* might leave people with a puzzled look on their faces but it certainly won't leave their heart unsure. Embedded deep within each of us is a longing for community. Every human being desires an ongoing experience of mutual relatedness with other human beings. We can't thrive without relationships that are meaningful, growing, and moving us toward who we were truly created to be. One of the most basic qualities of humans is the urge to be loved and to love others. There is hunger in all human beings to be welcomed into new and different relationships and to find a lasting bond in those relationships. We long for relationships that, on one hand, are capable of reliable common interaction and, on the other hand, have the same level of influence for a developing self-identity.

So, then, what exactly is community? How do we know where to find it? How do we know when we have found authentic community? What are the essential characteristics of a community—those that will make it bloom and flourish? What is each person's role within the community? These are incredibly important questions for gladhearted disciples. Gladhearted disciples are always looking for ways to plant a community where people can prosper. In order to plant a community where others can prosper, a more-than-basic understanding of community must be not only understood but also experienced. It is not the person who can live alone and depend only on himself or herself who is the personification of strength but the person who can learn to trust in the everyday good of others for his or her needs, individual progress, and sustainability.

A community, therefore, is a group of people that shares a similar outlook on life, has a similar collection of common interests, shares an overall vision for the reason the community exists and, more specifically, a set of goals or tasks that drive its future. Sound like a church made up of gladhearted disciples to you at all?

Beyond its organization, the components within a community also engage the heart and soul. This is where we get the term *community* from when we talk about what we desire for ourselves and others. We desire attachment to a story full of meaning, authority to contribute to the fulfillment of needs (both for self and for others), and continuous opportunities to express ourselves emotionally. Our identities develop within the community organization and the community's essence, which engages the heart and soul; we should avoid identity development in isolation or loneliness.

Nearly every week, at least three or four times, I am stopped in the hallways of my church and asked to help either a couple or a single person find a group. Most of my time is spent leading a team of people who spend the majority of their time launching groups related to spiritual growth and whose essence is belonging. The small groups, or communities, are designed to help people become deeply committed Christians. These communities are then "sent" out into everyday life—jobs, schools, neighborhoods, and so on—to live a missional life where their daily contact and interaction with nonreligious and nominally religious people make public God's presence. This is, in part, our evangelism strategy—to inspire, challenge, encourage, and equip our small groups to live into their various villages, towns, and cities to represent Jesus. We work hard to ensure our groups have the organization needed to launch (outlook on life, common interests, vision, goals, etc.) and the essence of true community (story, meaning, personal and communal needs met, etc.) to thrive.

We are created in the image and likeness of God. The creation narratives in Genesis help us understand that we are able to recognize God's authority and existence and the sacred kingdom in which we have been created to live in. We have intellect, emotion, freedom to make choices, and a competence to enter into deep relationships with God and others. We have the ability to live moral lives characterized by righteousness and devotion to God. These characteristics exist within each person God creates. These characteristics are the very matters that lead us to long for and hunger for a deep sense of community. We were made to share, to coinhabit, to be in healthy, intimate relationships with one another. When we are not in healthy, intimate relationships with others, we wither. The ongoing connection to others helps us flourish.

Living in community is so hard. Even though we were meant to live in community, our humanity makes it very difficult to live healthy and intimate lives with one another. Several times a year I am asked to attend a small-group gathering and mediate conflict because the group is not getting along or someone in the group is very hard to be around. But that is just it; if a community is meant as much for the other as for the self then the community must be for all people, even the ones who are hard to get along with. Most of the small groups in churches desire the organization but do not necessarily hold the same enthusiasm for the essence. Sometimes there are people in a group or community who don't exactly share all of the community's desire for organization and essence. However, true community is for everyone. Inclusivity, unity, diversity—these are all essential ingredients to a true community.

Sometimes I am asked in my role at our church if we have any affinity groups. We do have affinity groups, but they are not our goal. Our goal is to have groups of people who desire to become part of a group not merely because they all like golf or a certain kind of wine or a specific genre of movies. We dream of the day when groups form because people say, "I just want to create a place where everyone is welcomed and loved, regardless of affinity." To organize by affinity makes sense at times, for a season, and it can work to get groups started. However, affinity groups or communities that exist only for a certain reason or cause are by their very nature exclusive. A community ceases to be a community when it no longer makes itself accessible to those outside the community. Gladhearted disciples find a way to make community possible for all.

The reality is that a community isn't for you; it is with you. True community can only be attained, both in organization and in essence, when the people in the community choose to forgo being the primary person whose needs are met. Think about it for a minute. If everyone in your small group decided to give up his or her own personal desire to have his or her own needs met first, wouldn't every person's needs still be met by another? This is community—giving up your own self for the sake of the other so that you bring yourself to the community as a gift to serve others first. Community, both organization and essence, begins in our relationship to God, and there cannot be any personal hurdle to God's presence. This openness to God must also be openness to others, whether it is returned or not.[1] We offer ourselves to the community not expecting anything in return. If everyone did this, we'd all be overwhelmed with a sense of belonging, care, and love. This would be generosity at its best.

John Wesley, in one of his sermons, describes God's love as both "generous and disinterested."[2] God's love is generous in that there is absolutely no advantage to God—no praise or profit—not even the pleasure of loving. God loves not in order to get something in return but simply to love. God is love. Love is not a characteristic of God; love is God, if after all God is love.

Regarding Wesley's description of God's love as disinterested, I interpret that he means that God's love is unbiased by personal interest and that God's love does not have any particular affections in which it produces love. God's love is concerned with all affections, not one or two or three in particular. Wesley says that generous and disinterested love, when lived out by Christians, is the naked portraiture of a Christian. Gladhearted disciples strip down to the essentials—generosity and disinterest.

Communities in our churches that we launch and nurture should be filled with gladhearted disciples who live generously and with disinterest. Our small groups ought to be characterized by people who, even when there is no promise of love returned, choose to love in both structure and in essence of community. Our pastor Adam Hamilton has urged listeners, "Love, even if you don't feel like it. Love until you feel like loving."

There are certain practices that can help a community learn to live more like Wesley described God's love for us. These practices are not meant to be a formula by any stretch of the imagination. These practices can, however, truly lead toward a community that chooses to love generously and without interest toward any particular affection over another. Here are ten habits of communities that are on their way toward reflecting the nature of God:

1. Healing—restoring people back to one another and to self.

2. Discernment—listening for the Holy Spirit and the direction that the community should go in order to live into its purpose.

3. Forgiveness—letting go of any ill feelings; truly wishing the offender well.

4. Confession—sharing with one another the shortcomings of life. Coming clean with the things that might make it difficult to love generously and with a disinterest toward any particular person.

5. Sabbath—resting and remembering who God is and who we are not.

6. Sacredness—observing the sacred times and spaces in life. Looking for the thin veil that separates heaven and earth and finding ways to remember that holy moment.

7. Waiting—expectant waiting and preparation for the many wonderful things that God is going to do in and through the community.

8. Hospitality—the respect and love offered to all: stranger, friend, and neighbor.

9. Sharing—using the resources that others have (material goods, talents, gifts, expertise, and so on) to bless others.

10. Giving—to provide to those in need without the expectation to ever get anything back or for the provision to be compensated in some way.

Community is hard. In order to create environments for spiritual formation, however, gladhearted disciples do whatever it takes to allow people to connect to God, self, others, and the world, bringing their greatest joys and deepest sorrows and concerns as an expression and reminder of hope, believing that God is actively making all things new.

Chapter 5

Revisiting Christian Perfection

I am captivated with the idea of Christian perfection (also referred to as holy or perfect love). Since the first time I heard the phrase used I was fascinated by the proposal and the possibility. When I first heard the phrase I thought to myself, how could anyone ever be sinless? How is it even remotely possible that a person could be error-free? Is it actually possible to attain a state in which a person does not willfully sin? Could it be true that there are actual sins and simply mistakes? All of these and more questions have led me on a journey of discovering what Christian perfection is and how I might live a perfected life. This theological concept is a priority for gladhearted disciple making.

To this point in my discovery I can honestly say that I not only believe in Christian perfection—most Wesleyans do, by the way, which is why, in large part, they are Wesleyan—I believe that Christian perfection is the call for every human being. This, after all, was one of the central and differentiating tenets of not only John Wesley's theology but also Jesus's theology. Jesus didn't come just to die for us. Jesus also came to show us how to live. Jesus, then, is the model for a human being who can live a fully human life, a life of perfect love for God and others.

Christian perfection is, in short, a wholehearted love for God and all of creation. Christian perfection isn't isolated to an individual's own growth but, in its profound simplicity and also in its greatest complexity, is ultimately about an outward expression of love from self to others. John Wesley is known to have said that he knew of no holiness that was not social holiness. Christian perfection, therefore, must be attained through community formation. We must create environments for people to grow into maturity though fellowship, worship, discipleship, and mission. These four traits of maturity are the pillars of spiritual formation.

In my role at our church as one of the ministers of discipleship I am frequently asked about my view on Christian perfection. I am commonly asked questions like, "Do you really think we can become perfect?" or "Does being perfect mean that I don't make mistakes?" or "How am I supposed to understand what it means to be perfect?" These, and a host of other questions related to Christian perfection, are the fodder for great conversation. Gladhearted disciples believe in Christian perfection (or at the very least claim it to be a possibility) and are able to clearly articulate to others what it means to live a life of holy or perfected love. For this reason, we must endlessly revisit what Christian perfection is and what is required of us as disciples to live a perfected life.

It is important to deepen our conversation about Christian perfection by defining what we mean when use the term. Christian perfection means that the believer's heart is transformed and made capable of reaching a state in which the believer does not willfully sin. Said another way, within the life of the Christian there is no longer a voluntary disobedience and in its place within the heart—which was once ruled by love's perversion, sin—is a total, complete, and whole love for God and others. Christian perfection is reached by direction of the Holy Spirit. This holiness is only attainable through faith in Jesus Christ and is "nothing more, or less, than growing up in love and becoming a whole, complete human being made in the image of God as revealed by Jesus Christ."[1]

To believe, first, that Christian perfection is a realistic and worthwhile doctrine and, second, that the believer is capable of attaining Christian perfection, the believer must understand love. *Love* is a word that can mean anything, everything, or nothing. In this context, however, the gladhearted disciple understands love as what orders one's life—the realization that love is an orientation and it is the very thing that causes humankind to act, to relate, to speak, and to be. Love is the reason we exist. God is love and, therefore, we exist as humankind because God expressed God's desire to relate to humankind. In relating to humankind, God shows us what it means to order our life around God's intended ways as understood in God's revelation through Jesus Christ. All gladhearted disciples need to know, understand, and live by the idea that love is the central truth of the gospel.

A few years ago I came across an incredible book about Christian perfection called *A Theology of Love* by Mildred Bangs Wynkoop.[2] Wynkoop was an educator, missionary, and theologian. She was a Nazarene minister who changed the landscape of thinking on Christian perfection for many. One Nazarene pastor once told me he was going to leave the denomination until he read Wynkoop's book. Wynkoop changed the thinking from an idea based on legalism to an idea based solely on grace. Legalism, of course, is the rigid perspective on Christianity that presents the letter of the law in absence of a spirit of mercy. Grace, then, is the opposite. Grace is love and mercy given to us by God simply because God is love and God wants us to have it. Christian perfection, for so many, sadly, is rooted in a legalistic outlook on Christianity as opposed to an outlook born out of kindness and grace.

I have forever been changed by her book and look to it almost weekly as I seek to understand the disciple I am becoming as well as the best approach to teach the disciples I am shepherding.

Most of what follows in this particular chapter is a blend of Wynkoop's teaching on Christian perfection in her book and what I have come to understand in my own reading, studying, and living. Gladhearted disciples are people who strive toward perfect love—the complete and whole love for God and others. Gladhearted disciples seek not only the perfection of self, but the perfection of others.

Sometimes the best thing to do when trying to determine what something means is to identify first and foremost what something is not. To best understand Christian perfection let's first discover what it is not. Christian perfection is not:

- The void of temptation (even Jesus was tempted)

- The absence of ignorance or mistakes; an error-free life

- The absolute fulfillment of knowledge or understanding

- Rooted or ingrained in moralism and exclusions

- Protection from circumstances of systemic evil

- Protection from mental disorders or addictions

There are probably a host of other bullet points we could name. The list above is the issues I am most frequently asked about. In fact, in one of my Bible studies a person in the class raised her hand and said something to the effect, "So you are telling me that I can attain a state where I am guaranteed freedom from sin and disease?"

My reply was, "Um, no. That is exactly what I am not saying."

I went on to explain that perfection is not something that is finished or complete but something always transforming. It's a process and a journey. It is confusing for many because when we think of perfection we think of faultlessness or freedom from defect. Instead, when we speak of perfection, we are meaning to make perfect, as in a development or progression of maturation. Gladhearted disciples know the difference between faultlessness and what it means to be on their way toward being made whole.

So, then, what is Christian perfection if it isn't what we have identified above? Christian perfection is:

- **Pure love reigning above all else in the heart and life.** When love supersedes all other priorities, perfect love is attainable. When advantage to self is a priority, regardless of where it ranks on the list, Christian perfection is not a reasonable consideration.

- **When the entire will of God is the center of life.** People have come to me over the years and asked me, "How do I know what is the will of God for my life?" My response is always the same: "Do everything you can possibly do to reorient your life and all its priorities around your ongoing participation with God in restoring the world toward its intended wholeness." God is passionately and enduringly pursuing a restored relationship with humankind. As the church, God's people, gladhearted disciples, we are God's chosen agents of God's love and restoration. We are entirely living in the center of God's will when God's mission directs every aspect of our life.

- **What ought to be the case and can be so.** Gladhearted disciples understand and believe wholeheartedly that striving for Christian perfection is not the choice of the believer but is the calling of the believer. While *positional sanctification* (being set apart unto God in Christ) describes our standing in Christ as believers, and is typically understood to be an instantaneous work of God at the time of salvation, *practical sanctification* addresses the spiritual vitality as lived out in everyday life. Gladhearted disciples are optimistic people. They are also realistic people. They confess, or tell God the truth, regarding their shortcomings but at the same time lean into the resurrection truth that through the death, burial, and resurrection of Jesus all believers might live whole lives.

- **The factor that constitutes the work of the inner life with that of the outer life.** Christian perfection is what takes our missional instincts and turns them into missional expressions. It might be described by saying that our inward formation process points to the position of our heart (mind, soul, strength) while our outward formation process points to the posture we take when we demonstrate love with our body (hands, feet, voice, eyes, etc.). When lived in harmony, or in one accord, both the inward and outward aspects of missional discipleship assist us in moving toward a life of perfect love.

- **Where Jesus is Lord of all or not at all.** My son has a sign on his wall that reads, "Jesus Christ is Lord." He heard our pastor call our congregation to a life where Jesus is the Lord of our life, and since that sermon the phrase has remained on the wall in his bedroom. I asked my son one day, "Drew, do you know what that phrase means?" Drew responded by saying, "Yes. It means Jesus is either the King of our life or he isn't. It is really that simple, Dad." My son, Drew, is eleven. When we exclaim that Jesus is Lord, what we as gladhearted disciples are saying is that Jesus is the ultimate authority in all things—in every area of our life. He is King. He is the rightful ruler of our life and of this world. When we realize Christian perfection, Jesus must be the King of our life—all of it.

Finally, when it comes to Christian perfection, it is incredibly important to understand four key measurable implications. Measurable implications or metrics are very hard to gauge when it comes to spiritual formation. We don't make and sell widgets; we cultivate and send disciples as church leaders. Widgets would be much easier to measure. How many did we make? How much did it cost us to make them? How much did we sell them for? How many did we sell? Bang. Answer those four questions and you have concise, clear, and compelling metrics. We can't do that with disciple making. Most of what we would try and measure we cannot see since it involves the interior life. Yes, sure, we can see how someone lives their outward life (attitude, spirit, service, etc.) but in order to live whole the inner life and the outer life must be working in harmony.

There are things, however, we can do as gladhearted disciple makers that can help inspire, encourage, challenge, and equip disciples toward Christian perfection. Four measurable implications for gladhearted disciple making are:

- **Teaching and presenting an accurate and adequate view of God.** God is not small, and to teach God as though you have God figured out (removing the mystery and the spirituality of theology) makes God seem small. Also, to neglect holiness teaching is to not present an accurate and adequate view of God. God desires humanity to be whole. To teach anything but a personal and social holiness is to ignore God's command to be holy. Gladhearted disciples present God's desire for holiness. This commanded wholeness, by the way, is not merely for our own piety . . . it is for the sake of the world.

- **Unwavering commitment and faith in the person, work, and ministry of Jesus.** Jesus showed us how to live a holy life—a life of voluntarily giving up self for the sake of the world. Jesus said really cool things, yes. Jesus did really cool things, yes. Jesus taught using really cool metaphors, yes. Jesus loved using really cool means, yes. Yes. Yes. Yes. Jesus, however, is the way, the truth, and the life. Pastor and author Eugene Peterson once noted in his book *The Jesus Way*, "Jesus is the way of salvation. We follow his way. Jesus is the way of eternal life. We follow his way. The way Jesus does it is the way we do it. Jesus is the way we come to God. Period. End of discussion."[3] Jesus, therefore, is the way we understand what it means to live a life of perfect love. To leave Jesus out of your thinking, listening, being, and doing is to lose your way on the journey toward Christian perfection.

- **Relational or social holiness is the way we best understand Jesus.** Jesus isn't the way in isolation. Jesus is the way in community. The Word became human and lived among us. Gladhearted disciples know and teach with their whole heart the importance of growing toward maturity in the midst of others—even people who are hard to like. Jesus came and moved into the neighborhood. He didn't build a palace in the mountains overlooking the city. Instead, Jesus pitched a tent among the people, the marginalized, and presented himself as the way, the truth, and the life.

- **Biblical, cultural, and personal provision for a holy life.** God, through the gift of God's Son Jesus Christ and the direction of the Holy Spirit, gives us everything we need to move toward Christian perfection. The scriptures teach and guide us, our lives give us experience testing the scriptures, and our individual contexts provide us the culture in which to live relationally. If we are to be people of wholeness, or people marked by a holy love, we are to be people who look to God and what God provides for us to live into our relatedness. Remember, we are created in the image of God. We are created to live a fully human life.

I conclude this chapter with the words of John Wesley:

> Let your soul be filled with so entire a love to him, that you may love nothing but for his sake. Have a pure intention of heart, a steadfast regard to his glory in all your actions. . . . For then, and not till then, is that mind in us, which was also in Christ Jesus, when in every motion of our heart, in every word of our tongue, in every work of our hands, we pursue nothing but in relation to him, and in subordination to his pleasure; when we, too, neither think, nor speak, nor act, to fulfill our own will, but the will of him that sent us; when whether we eat or drink, or whatever we do, we do it to all the glory of God.[4]

This is the call of the gladhearted disciple. So be it.

Part Three

Gladhearted Disciples and Their Embodied Practice

Chapter 6

The Gospel of Peace and Justice

I recently did an informal survey of several of the small groups in our church. I discovered that when most of the people in some of our small groups think about the creation narratives found in Genesis 1–2, they typically think of (1) what God created, (2) what days God created, and (3) how long it took God to create. These three common thoughts can lead Christians away from the originally intended understanding and direction of the creation stories. More central to the Christian faith than the three typical essential views above and the micro details of creation are the macro concepts of the overarching relationships and the condition of those relationships before Genesis 3, when love is perverted and sin enters the world.

Embedded into the creation narratives we discover four principal relationships. (1) There is a relationship between God and humans. (2) Humanity has a relationship with self. (3) Humans have a relationship with one another. (4) Finally, humans have a relationship with God, self, and others all within the greater cosmos. These four narratives interact throughout the rest of the Christian story. From Genesis 3 to Revelation 22, the four relationships of God, self, others, and the world persist in progression. Admittedly, the progress of these four relationships is, at times, intermittent and categorically incomplete. The essence, however, of each of these four relationships prior to Genesis 3 and the perversion of love, is twofold. The essence of these relationships is peace and justice.

By *peace* I do not merely mean the absence of conflict, mental calm, or tranquility. While those three and other characteristics of a peaceful world existed I do not believe them to be the chief characterization of the world.

By *peace* I mean harmony, accord, or shalom. *Shalom* is more than a Jewish greeting for coming and going. *Shalom* means "complete." *Shalom* means "whole." Therefore, the four relationships of God, self, others, and the world are marked first and foremost by God's intended desire for wholeness. Prior to Genesis 3 and the choice of Adam and Eve to rebel against God, usurping God's authority, there was a world characterized by wholeness, unity, and fullness.

By *justice* I mean that the world, being whole, was in no need of correction. If we think of justice as the righting of wrongs, then there would be no reason for justice prior to Genesis 3, accept as an intrinsic characteristic of God. There was no animosity between God and humans. There was no one without the essential needs of love, food, shelter, and care. According to our creation stories there was union between God and humans, serenity with self, intimacy between humans, and a comprehensive sense of enjoyment of the natural world. There was no need for justice of any kind. God was just and, therefore, the universe in its entirety was a place of purpose (to worship God and represent God as co-caretakers), moral exactness, and fairness.

This is the way that God intended the world and all that is within it to function. God set up the world for lasting peace and justice to reign. This is not only what God desired for the world upon creation but also what God desires for the world today. God longs for the day when all will be made new and the original intention in which the world was created will again reign in lasting peace and justice.

Once I was talking to a new friend of mine named Jeff who had just begun attending our church. He saw a story on the local news about hundreds of high school students who lined the street across from our church in the late spring of 2014, blocking people who were protesting at a funeral. It struck Jeff, through the actions of high school students, that our church was a place motivated by and striving for peace and justice. Rather than violently shouting back to the group of protesters these students stood quietly and gently holding signs that said simply, "love wins." He saw the images on the Internet and decided he would come to Resurrection and check it out. Jeff is new to the faith and exploring God with a dedication and enthusiasm that is contagious. Before he was relocated to another state for a job, Jeff would regularly text me during our senior pastor's sermons asking questions and agreeing with his preaching by making statements like, "Yes! Yes! Yes!" Jeff came to our church because deeply embedded in his soul was a longing for a world full of peace and justice. This, after all, is the gospel story. The gospel is the grand story of God's will, way, and work of providing peace (salvation) and justice for all of humanity through the gift of God's son, Jesus Christ.

One day while talking with Jeff about a recent sermon Jeff asked something like, "So this is what the church is all about? The church is meant to be a place of peace and justice?"

"Yes, Jeff," I said. "The church is the extension of God's love in the world designed to participate with God to restore the world toward its intended wholeness."

Jeff fired back, "So God didn't make the world to be filled with hate and violence and inequality?"

"Quite the opposite, Jeff," I remarked. "In fact, God made the world whole and the people of the earth have been invited by God to make the world right again."

"That's not religion, that's a revolution!" Jeff exclaimed.

Jeff is right. God's mission to restore the world toward its intended wholeness is a revolution. God is raising up a generation of people who are committed to peace and justice in this world. Gladhearted disciples are people who accept the invitation and find methods and mediums in which to live into God's mission by living lives characterized by peace and justice.

The Christian story, the gospel, which is provided for us in overflowing and rich pages of the Bible, is a story of a God who, by God's very nature, is redeeming the world. For those of us who live with the hope that comes from the resurrection, the disunion created between God and humans, the endless shame humans place on self, the constant blame that humans place on one another, and the destructive patterns of the universe so profoundly intense in the Genesis 3 narrative of wrongdoing are fading away because of the gospel. Gladhearted disciples know that they are presently living in a world that is broken but redeemable. Gladhearted disciples know that through the birth, life, death, burial, resurrection, and ascension of Jesus there is the possibility for reunion between God and humans. Gladhearted disciples also know that peace with self, others, and the world is not only plausible but also wholeheartedly promised through the salvific work of God though Jesus.

This four-storied narrative found in the creation stories changes the way that gladhearted disciples choose to live their lives. Gladhearted disciples are alert to the changing cultures around them and look for immediate and enduring ways to make peace and provide justice. Peace and justice must be made. They must be continually generated and formed. Peace and justice can only be made at the speed in which the church, full of gladhearted disciples, chooses to proclaim and preserve the very peace that sustains Godlike life. Gladhearted disciples make peace at every moment, choosing to give up what makes them feel "right" for the good of the kingdom. Giving up what we think is right is not living without conviction and belief. On the contrary, giving up what we think is right in order to receive the other, regardless of how lofty, strange, or out of place another's worldview might be, is making peace. Furthermore, giving up what we think is right in order to live peacefully may very well be one of the most important convictions we can hold. This doesn't mean that people aren't wrong. It does mean, however, that you give up the privilege to prove you are right.

Gladhearted disciples educate toward peace and justice. Our churches must be filled with disciples who are increasingly passionate about inspiring, challenging, encouraging, and equipping the emerging generations to make peace and exercise justice for the common good in the ideal of the kingdom of God (think specifically about the Sermon on the Mount and Sermon on the Plain in Matthew and Luke, respectively). This means that the church must continue to find ways to invent peace and justice. Peace and justice cannot be passive or dictatorial. Peace and justice that reek of dominance and oppression are of course not peace or justice at all. We don't force peace and justice on others. Instead we model what it means to make peace and justice, or wholeness, in the name of Jesus, with every ounce of energy and passion we have. After all, what generates peace and justice? Peace and justice generate peace and justice, and the only way to have a world filled with peace and justice is to trust one another and first form a passion for peace and justice within the interior of our lives. Inner peace and justice beget exterior peace and justice. Gladhearted disciples are seeking ways to live at peace and provide justice for all of mankind by first shaping it within. Clearly, then, the way to peace and justice for all gladhearted disciples is reconciliation. This is the way God has set up the church. God has set up the church as a force of reconciliation where God is using you and me and all of the peoples of the earth to bring forth peace and justice. Gladhearted disciples are agents of reconciliation. This is our purpose and chief ministry initiative both personally and communally—to present Jesus as the way to salvation (Rom 5:10-11; 2 Cor 5:18-19)—making an appeal to the world through lives that demonstrate and are characterized by wholeness. Through Jesus's death, peace with God, self, others, and the world is made real. Gladhearted disciples live into their calling and make peace and generate justice initiatives that remind the world that God has not forgotten them.

Chapter 7

Creating "Do You Remember When?" Stories

I'd much rather hear the words, "do you remember when" as opposed to the words, "let me tell you a story." Don't get me wrong, I love hearing a good story, but I would much rather reflect on a shared experience with a family member, friend, colleague, or parishioner than concentrate on someone else's story. The words, "do you remember when" imply something much more significant than the words, "let me tell you a story." "Let me tell you a story" is certainly an invitation into an experience and at some level also an invitation into meaning.[1] However, the words, "do you remember when" imply an invitation to reflect on meaning already established though a mutual occurrence or encounter.

A few weeks ago I was speaking at a conference for pastors and church leaders in Atlanta. Several of the friends I went to college with were in attendance. After one of my workshops we went out for dinner. Before long it was midnight, and we were asked to leave the restaurant since the staff was tired of waiting on us and wanted to go home. The conversation continued when we all got back to the hotel lobby. We stayed up until 2:00 a.m. telling "do you remember when" stories. In the morning my stomach was sore from laughing so hard. My heart, however, was full and felt great because the stories had taken me back to some of the most formative years of my life. Who I was in that very moment was part of how my experience with those friends, even twenty years earlier, had shaped me. I found meaning in those stories, and so did my friends. In fact the reason we spent the time the night before laughing was because it meant something significant to all of us. Stories, especially the ones we share with others, make meaning and give our lives direction. It is the laughter, pain, tears, triumphs, and doubt that we share with others that connect us to humanity and move us to be generous people who are on our way toward deepening our understanding of life.

In his book *Tell Me a Story*, Daniel Taylor suggests that stories are the currency of human interchange.[2] He goes on to say that, "Stories turn mere chronology, one thing after another, into the purposeful action of plot, and thereby into meaning." I couldn't agree more. Story, whether telling one or listening to one or living in one, gives us a connection to God, self, others, and the world that few other things, if any, can provide. Stories put us in touch with others because stories are interwoven and we "cannot live our story alone because we are characters in each other's story."[3]

Gladhearted disciples recognize that story is a currency for connection and community. They recognize that stories bring us together and connect us to one another's world. Gladhearted disciples live by the reality of story and because of that choose to find ways to create "do you remember when" moments that allow people to experience deep, growing, and lasting community. After all, through story we link past, present, and future. Story tells where we are and where we are going as a people, as a church. Our shared stories tell us that without a doubt there is a place for me, for you, for us.[4]

Churches that desire to make meaning for people by sharing experiences, thus creating shared narratives, are intentional about the experiences. They don't just hold events or provide spaces. On the contrary, churches and congregations of generous and enduring disciples create experiences to engage nonreligious people. Gladhearted disciples primarily rely on four key elements for forming people through story: (1) invitation, (2) participation, (3) contribution, and (4) imagination.

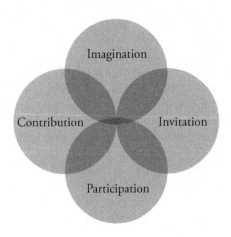

Invitation: It may be simple, perhaps it almost seems simplistic, but the reality is as I travel around the country and talk with churches who inquire about how they might engage nonreligious people with the gospel they seldom, if ever, actually invite anyone from the community to join them.

I once asked a pastor, "So how are you inviting people to attend these community events?"

His response was, "I'm actually not sure." He turned to one of his staff and asked, "How are we inviting people?"

The staff person replied with a shrug of the shoulders as if to say, "I have no idea."

I can guarantee you this much: if you aren't inviting people and welcoming them to engage your communitywide, church-led, or facilitated initiatives, they aren't coming. Will your nonreligious neighbors ever attend your church service or anything your church does if you don't invite them? Of course, inviting them is just the beginning. We also, as gladhearted disciples, have to welcome them into our community, as they are, knowing they may not want anything we have to offer but at the same time being authentically who we are. Part of welcoming people to share experiences with you, thus creating "do you remember when" stories, is not pretending to be someone you are not. Be real from the beginning and you won't have any surprises later.

Participation: In order to create experiences that lead to "do you remember when" stories, you need more than an invitation. You need to create opportunities for people to participate in something. John Wimber, one of the founders of the Vineyard Movement, once said, "If you want people to come to church, give them a job." I think that participation is a critical element that leads toward the kind of shared experiences that are going to become stories that are told over and over again. Think about it for a minute. Let's say that a spectator at the game is telling you how that particular team pulled the game out in the end. Is that as powerful as one of the players telling you how they won the game? Better yet, what if you are one of the players years later running into a teammate saying, "Do you remember when we pulled out the win against whoever?" Now which is more powerful? To engage the story of God, people best respond to participating in the story of God through mission trips, justice initiatives, acts of kindness, and so on. Organize communitywide initiatives that invite people to participate with us and in doing so participate with God (maybe not even knowing it until some days, months, or years later).

Contribution: Of course we can give people an invitation and find ways for them to participate in God's mission, but if they don't realize the contribution they are making or the significance of what they are doing then it may seem like mere busy work. Let me give you an example of what I mean. Since I have been on staff at our church I have witnessed what it means to allow people to contribute in meaningful ways. Our church has given the entire offering at our Christmas Eve services to carefully selected (through an application and discernment process) organizations and/or causes. Each year one of the causes is a local initiative and the other is a global initiative. As I am sure is true at your church, we have many visitors who attend our Christmas Eve services. If you attend one of our Christmas Eve services you are invited to participate in making a tremendous contribution. People know that they are more than participants by being in attendance and by being asked to give—they are contributors to something way bigger than any one person or organization could ever do on their own. In 2014 we gave away over a million dollars to several great causes! Yes, I think it has a lot to do with people feeling generous at Christmas. However, I think it has way more to do with the opportunity that they are being given to work with other people to contribute to something big to make an even bigger difference in the lives of people.

Imagination: I've worked for various churches for most of my adult life. I've found that one of the church's greatest challenges is consistently firing the imagination of people, giving them a picture of what could be. Visionaries, in the church especially, are very unique. I am not talking about people with good ideas. Rather, I am talking about people who have the ability to cast a vision for people of the way the future could be. Gladhearted disciples must become people who can paint what it looks like for heaven and earth to collide. Gladhearted disciples must help other maturing disciples imagine the possibility and power of the story in which they are living. The story that God and humans paint in the scripture, for the way the world ought to be and could be, is the model for us today. Jesus, the model of life and ministry, fires the imagination of his disciples and of an entire nation. Jesus calls it the kingdom of God, or the kingdom of heaven. Gladhearted disciples can see it. They know what it takes to move their life and their spheres of influence (friends, coworkers, family, neighbors) toward earth as it is in heaven. The imagination gives people the ability to discover and sustain what might otherwise simply just be fleeting experiences. Gladhearted disciples develop the ability to fire the imagination of people, giving them the ability to:

- See a new hope or alternative reality

- Provide new significance to old truths

- Change the way they view the world, showing them how faith and life intersect

- Cultivate new commitments to newfound spiritual discoveries

- Feed the soul with creative and artistic expressions of God's work in the world

- Provide the way for unseen matters of faith to be on equal footing with seen matters of faith

The imagination is crucial for engaging people in gladhearted discipleship. Gladhearted disciples are committed to painting a picture of the way the world could be—a world not only described by Jesus but also lived by Jesus. I believe the scriptures, the word of God, are most fully alive when activated through the lives of gladhearted disciples.

We live in a world full of stories of God, self, others, and the world. Stories are the central way in which people make meaning and find community. All great stories have a storyteller, a compelling plot, and an audience. Gladhearted disciples are intentional about engaging nonreligious and nominally religious people through invitation, participation, contribution, and imagination, creating "do you remember when" stories that make meaning for people. These stories allow people to find Christian community where they discover their lives interwoven with the narrative of God. Gladhearted disciples provide experiences for people to embrace a story that is larger, more dramatic, and more intense than any other story they know. It's the story of God—a story of redemption and restoration for the whole world. Gladhearted disciples see stories inside of the story and find God's mission to restore the world to its intended wholeness.

Chapter 8

Understanding the Reason
and Role of the Church

A fter one of our services, a young boy probably around the age of eleven or twelve asked me, "Do you have a favorite prayer?" Before I could respond, this boy said, "I kind of like The Lord's Prayer."
I replied, "Oh yeah. Cool. Why that prayer?"

His short response was, "Because it tells me what to do."

On the drive home I was reflecting on my conversation with this boy. I began thinking of prayers we find in the Bible that I hold on to for my daily growth. Along with The Lord's Prayer, an important one is Jesus's prayer while on the cross, "Father, forgive them, for they don't know what they're doing" (Luke 23:34). That particular prayer is essential for understanding the whole of the atoning work of Jesus on the cross. Another prayer for daily growth and living is the benediction prayer of Jude 1:2, which says, "May you have more and more mercy, peace, and love." The prayer of Job is captivating. Job has just experienced tremendous tragedy and pain and falls to the ground in worship saying, "Naked I came from my mother's womb; naked I will return there. The LORD has given; the LORD has taken; bless the LORD's name" (1:21).

There are hundreds of prayers throughout the scriptures and throughout the history of the church that guide, challenge, and equip us for daily living, loving, and leading. However, no prayer ranks higher than the prayer that is widely referred to as the Prayer of All Prayers. It is the prayer of Jesus found in chapter 17 of the Gospel of John. This prayer sets the tone for the reason and role of the church. Gladhearted disciples see this particular prayer of Jesus as the guiding remembrance of the very reason God has sent Jesus to set apart a people who will represent God to the world. John 17 clearly shapes the reason and role of the church. It certainly isn't the only passage in scripture that points to the reason and role of the disciple; however, it does, directly from the lips of Jesus, help us know Jesus's desire for his disciples and the entire world.

I will not exegete the prayer in great detail. However, for summary and context's sake, let's look at three sections to this prayer. First, Jesus prays for himself (John 17:1-5). This isn't actually a prayer for Jesus but a prayer for the Father. Jesus, above all else, wishes to bring glory to God through the completion of God's mission. This should not surprise us; Jesus is all about the glory of God.

In the second section of this prayer (John 17:6-19), Jesus prays for his disciples. The gist of Jesus's prayer here is that God would continue to protect his disciples by protecting them from "the evil one." Jesus desires for the disciples to be sanctified, or set apart, in order that they might be present and illumined in the world but far removed from the darkness the evil one revels in. It is important in this section of the prayer to also note that Jesus claims that he is sending the disciples into the world, just as God has sent him into the world. This is a direct connection to God's sending nature as a missionary God. Gladhearted disciples recognize they are sent into the world not to take on the characteristics of the world but instead to reveal the nature of God through their sanctified lives.

Finally, the third major section of this prayer concerns itself with all future believers. Jesus prays for the church, the kingdom society that is emerging as a different kind of people to carry out God's mission as seen through the life, death, burial, resurrection, and ascension of Jesus. His prayer in this section (John 17:20-26) is twofold. First, Jesus prays that all disciples would be one, as Jesus and God are one. Jesus's prayer is for them to be "made completely one," and this prayer isn't just to make the disciples feel good about their own community. Instead, Jesus desires for the church to be one in order that it might reveal to the world that God truly did send Jesus. Second, Jesus's prayer is "so that" the world might know. Several times throughout this prayer Jesus placed the two words "so" and "that" together in order to help us, the church, know that we are not a community turned inward but a growing inward community to be turned outward not for our own sake but for the sake of the world. Gladhearted disciples know that they are people whose spiritual life isn't for their own personal piety but for the sake of the world. If the church doesn't end all of its sentences with the phrase "for the sake of the world," then it has lost its way. The reason the church exists is for the sake of the world. The role of the church is to be one—a place of community—where the mission and message of Jesus Christ mark the community. This means, then, that the church is meant for conversion. Its purpose it the ongoing conversion of a community whose goal it is to see a conversion in the lives of the people of this earth—on earth as it is in heaven. By conversion I mean a true renovation of the soul, heart, mind, and body of the church in which evangelism, hospitality, generosity, liberation, and so on mark the church as a people existing for the sake of the world so that "the world will know that you [God] sent me" (John 17:23). The church is meant to be a community where nonreligious and nominally religious people are becoming deeply committed Christians, for the sake of the world.

This means that gladhearted disciples recognize their role and reason as a community of people, living on mission, to intentionally, strategically, and faithfully make a new culture—a kingdom culture. Gladhearted disciples witness to the person and work of Jesus, for the sake of the world, by creating a culture marked by kingdom attributes, as revealed by Jesus. Among other attributes, gladhearted disciples are people and communities that:

1. **Tell God the truth.** In order to change the culture around us, or better yet to make a new culture, gladhearted disciples know that utter honesty to God (confession) marks for us our own shortcomings and at the same time awakens us to forgiveness. Telling God the truth about our lives means that we are accepting responsibility for what we have done and who we are. The first step of people and faith communities making a new culture is to come out of hiding and face reality for our lives and the lives of those around us.[1]

2. **Think critically and thoughtfully.** I am amazed at the number of people who claim truth solely on what another has told them. For many, the truths of the Bible are held as personal virtues not because they have investigated the scriptures themselves but because somewhere along the way someone told them something that someone else told them may possibly be true. Gladhearted disciples who wish to make a new culture recognize the importance of thinking critically—reflective and reasonable thinking.[2] Gladhearted disciples don't take someone's word for it and pass it on as truth without determining the authenticity, accuracy, and worth of the proposed truth.[3] Gladhearted disciples wonder, calculate, adapt, grasp, invent, generalize, and so on in order to develop a set of convictions and beliefs to live by. This means, as disciples, we engage in meaningful conversation that is thoughtful and intellectually stimulating.

3. **Live as an illustration of truth.** Gladhearted disciples make culture by creating and sustaining a way of life characterized by engaging in authentic community, seeking to do what is right or living our God's intended ways, and developing a desire for ongoing conversion. We increase the frequency and duration of the holy moments of our life, and love our brothers and sisters, even the ones we don't agree with. We confess Jesus with our actions of mercy, compassion, and grace.

4. **Live as a healer.** Gladhearted disciples are alert to the needs of those around them and live in consistent pursuit of remedying those very needs. The gladhearted disciple is a healer who brings pastoral care and treatment through delivering hope, dignity, value, and justice. We might call this a "bigger than me" perspective on life—a kingdom perspective if you will—where being a humble presence is priority. Gladhearted disciples slow down their life enough to recognize the needs of others and to respond swiftly and appropriately. Jesus modeled this better than anyone. Jesus's ministry of listening and presence (not just proximity) allowed him to meet people where they were and at the same time help them get beyond the place holding them captive by oppression or possession.

5. **Tell stories of God's transformation.** Gladhearted disciples participate with God's mission to restore the world toward its intended wholeness by sharing and showing the life-giving message of the gospel through compassionate action and kind, winsome, and truthful words. Acts 1:8 is very clear. Just after teaching disciples about the kingdom of God for forty days, Jesus tells his disciples to stay in Jerusalem and wait for the gift of the Spirit. The Gospel of John 14–16, in particular, reveals to us that Jesus has already told his disciples about the Holy Spirit, and now they are to sit and wait for the gift to arrive. When the gift arrives, Jesus tells them, the power of the Spirit will be on the disciples to tell the story of God. Gladhearted disciples are storytellers who deliver the context and meaning of Jesus and the gospel by bearing witness to God's mission. We, as gladhearted disciple makers, are called to equip our people to become storytellers to tell God's story to a world that doesn't see a beginning or end to God's great narrative yet hungers to become a part of something bigger.

6. **Serve others as a porter.** Saint Benedict's Rule says, "Let all guests be welcomed as Christ."[4] Gladhearted disciples make a new culture by welcoming guests and strangers into the community. A life-shaping book by George Hunter III called *The Celtic Way of Evangelism* paints a picture of a welcome-minded gladhearted disciple in this way:

> Put yourself in the place of a seeker, a refugee, or an abused teenager who has been invited to visit a monastic community, and you have found your way there. What would you likely experience? You would meet a "porter" stationed near the monastic community's entrance, whose chief role is to welcome guests and introduce them to the rest of the community.[5]

Gladhearted disciples seek to be porters, positioning themselves near the church community, welcoming all peoples as guests and introducing them to the community. If we want to make a new culture we must rethink the way in which we engage the nonreligious and nominally religious. We cannot merely proclaim with words; we must help people find community and become one, which was the prayer of Jesus in John 17. Gladhearted disciples welcome everyone as Christ and create environments of space, trust, tolerance, invitation, peace, and order where all guests have a chance to experience the oneness Christ so desires for this world.

If the church is about conversion, and the way toward conversion is for the Christian community to make a new culture marked by kingdom virtues, then gladhearted disciples are curating Christianity. We are custodians of The Way that help people discover meaning, truth, and mystery in environments built on authentic community.

The church is the express agency that God has created and sustained over all of these hundreds and hundreds of years to deliver the message of wholeness found in Jesus. Gladhearted disciples preserve, by co-caretaking with God, the mission that restores the world toward its intended wholeness.

Part Four

GLADHEARTED DISCIPLES AND THEIR COMMITMENT TO YIELDED GUIDANCE

Chapter 9

Catching the Wind: The Holy Spirit and the Gladhearted Disciple

T he father of one of my childhood friends had a sailboat. Occasionally we'd find a summer day when we would untie it from the dock, shove off, and try to make something out of what might ordinarily be a rather mundane day. We really had no idea what we were doing. We knew this much: without a sail to catch the wind, we were going to have a hard time of making it a memorable day. I know next to nothing about sailing but I do know that if you are not able to catch the wind, you'll go nowhere. The Christian life is like this. If you don't recognize the power of the Holy Spirit and harness the Spirit for your life and the life of your entire community, you'll likely go nowhere as a person or as a people.

The Holy Spirit is the power and presence of God. The Holy Spirit is what gives life to believers and their communities. The Holy Spirit is the very "breath" and "wind" that allows believers and communities of believers to realize the oneness that Jesus prays for in John 17. Gladhearted disciples recognize the Holy Spirit as an agent of creation, the source of inspiration and power, and the manifestation of God's presence. The Holy Spirit represents the company and the activity of God and the enduring presence of Jesus in the church. The Spirit, as promised by Jesus, not only empowers gladhearted disciples for the purpose of the church within God's mission of restoration for all but also provides the spiritual compass that shapes the formation of all believers. Gladhearted disciples know beyond a shadow of a doubt that the Holy Spirit, the divine power and presence of God, is the core of the church's existence and sustenance.

The shortest way I know how to describe the story of God or the story-line of the Bible is to say it this way: God the Father sends God the Son. God the Son sends God the Holy Spirit. God the Holy Spirit sends the church into the world to bear witness to the ongoing redemptive work of God in the world. We, as gladhearted disciples, are sent into the world and given power by the Spirit to bear witness or represent God to the world through our lives. Gladhearted disciples are the agents of God's deliverance or salvation. God chooses to fulfill God's mission through human beings. This means that we must first and foremost make ourselves available to be sent into the world. Gladhearted disciples open their minds, hearts, and hands and say, "Here am I" and allow room for the Holy Spirit in all of its mystery to use them in whatever way the Holy Spirit so chooses. It is hard for many of us to comprehend but the reality is this: we have the same transforming and enlivening power of the Holy Spirit available to us that Jesus has available to him. We are communities of people awaiting the ministry of the Spirit to use us for reconciliation purposes. As we deliver this ministry of reconciliation we are expectant people waiting for the world to change around us.

In the book of Acts we clearly see the role of the Spirit in guiding a community of believers into the ministry of reconciliation. Craig Van Gelder, in his fine book *The Ministry of the Missional Church: A Community Led by the Spirit*, gives readers five dimensions of the Spirit's ministry.[1] I will summarize and provide commentary on Van Gelder's five dimensions, hopefully making a sturdy case for the way in which communities of gladhearted disciples should expect the Holy Spirit to be their guiding presence and governing power. Van Gelder has captured five key aspects that ought to help leaders and congregations refocus, refuel, and reimagine their purpose and priorities.

1. **The Holy Spirit forms people into a new society through the redemption provided by Jesus Christ and, therefore, gives them a new identity—an identity founded and sustained in the life and ministry of Jesus.** Through the ministry of the Holy Spirit, glad-hearted disciples are made into a community of people who no longer are consumed with the needs of self. Instead, the Holy Spirit calls people into a community or society that is marked by generosity. A generous community is a group of people who find their identity in giving to others and for others without any regard as to whether or not there is

any commensurate return. As we have discussed in other places in this book, gladhearted disciples are generous people. They place their needs behind the needs of the others around them. In doing so, the needs of all in the community are cared for. The Holy Spirit renarrates a community by marking it with the ministry and message of Jesus.

2. **The Holy Spirit provides, equips, and empowers leaders to guide these new societies.** I've always been fascinated with the part of Acts chapter 1 near the end when Peter realizes that, as prophecy has told, the disciples need to replace Judas. The scripture says that they need a person who was with Jesus from the time of his baptism all the way to his ascension. Essentially, then, they are going to replace Judas with a leader who is ready to lead based on the fact that he spent enough time with Jesus to understand the mission and the call to lead within that community. There are names of two men put forth who meet the qualifications. These two men are Joseph called Barsabbas (also known as Justus) and Matthias. The disciples lean into the direction of the Holy Spirit, praying for the discernment needed. They draw straws or cast lots, and Matthias is chosen. Matthias is added to the eleven sent ones and is now a leader of leaders and gladhearted disciple maker. Have you ever wondered how two people could be ready to lead along with the eleven apostles and never even be mentioned in the four gospels? The Holy Spirit was already at work in the lives of Justus and Matthias. Long before they were needed to replace Judas, the Holy Spirit was preparing these men for such a mission as spreading the message of the gospel. This is how the Holy Spirit works—mysteriously and sometimes even clandestinely preparing disciples to be leaders for God's mission. Not only does the Spirit call leaders, the Spirit empowers them with courage, strength, wisdom, grace, mercy, and so on to lead faithfully and generously. Listen up, gladhearted disciple makers! Even now the Holy Spirit is preparing the people you are discipling to carry the mission of God into the community in contextual ways.

3. **The Holy Spirit guides these leaders, and the entire community they lead, into sanctified living that reflects their new identity in Jesus Christ.** The Holy Spirit calls people out of their former selves and converts them into their new selves. This is conversion and this is the goal of the Christian mission—to repent of our sins and be

on our way to holy love, transformed by the renewing of our minds. Taking on the life of Jesus, we, as gladhearted disciples, are led by the Holy Spirit to be a community living in the presence and power of the risen Christ. Theologian Jürgen Moltmann once wrote, "the church is the hope in the world's 'valley of the shadow'; that is the messianic people of God, who remain true to the suffering earth, because they expect the 'new earth' in which righteousness dwells. This church is about more than religion; it is about new life. This church is about more than the church; it is about the Kingdom of God. This church is about more than men and women; it is about reconciliation of the cosmos."[2] This, friends, is the reason the Holy Spirit guides us toward sanctified lives. We are guided into sanctified lives so that we might first and foremost be concerned with the needs of this world. This concern (restoration of the cosmos, to use Moltmann's words) is what marks us and identifies us with Jesus. We are led by the Spirit into sanctification for the sake of the world.

4. **The Holy Spirit guides these leaders and communities into missional work or work that participates with God's mission toward its intended wholeness, in contextual ways.** As I have stated in numerous places throughout this book, God's mission is to restore the world toward its intended wholeness. Without question, the church, as led by the Holy Spirit, is guided into the world to contextualize the gospel message. Said differently, the Holy Spirit leads us to understand the heritages, customs, beliefs, traditions, and so on of a place and to make the gospel real within that place, respectfully and honorably. Every place has a story, and God has already been where the place is. Gladhearted disciples know that every place God takes them by the guidance of the Holy Spirit is a place where we join God; we don't bring God. Therefore, our task as gladhearted disciple makers is to help our disciples understand that the nature of the mission of God includes three integrative aspects, namely, the biblical story, the cultural story, and the congregational story. Remove one of these three aspects and the mission isn't relevant to God's mission. It is where these three aspects intersect that God desires to express God's heart. Gladhearted disciples make meaning out of their story, the story of God, and the story of culture, providing a contextual gospel that penetrates the darkness of this world with the light of the living Jesus. The Holy Spirit makes this all possible. The Holy Spirit transfers the spiri-

tual life and power of Jesus to God's people through baptism and indwelling. This results in believers being in Jesus and Jesus being in them, and all believers pull together to form the body of Christ, which serves as Jesus's body on earth. Saint Teresa of Avila once said, "Christ has no body but yours, / No hands, no feet on earth but yours, / Yours are the eyes with which he looks / with compassion on this world, / Yours are the feet with which he walks to do good, / Yours are the hands, with which he blesses all the world. / Yours are the hands, yours are the feet, / Yours are the eyes, you are his body. / Christ has no body now but yours, / No hands, no feet on earth but yours, / Yours are the eyes with which he looks / with compassion on this world. / Christ has no body now on earth but yours."[3]

5. **The Holy Spirit directs these leaders and communities into the broken world to "unbreak" the world through suffering by extending mercy and exercising justice.** A few weeks ago my daughter asked me if I had any money. I said, "No. I gave my last twenty bucks to a homeless guy earlier."

"Cool," she said.

One of my sons overheard me tell my daughter that and he said, "Why did you give away your last twenty bucks?"

I responded by saying, "I felt the Holy Spirit tell me to give it away."

"I don't even know what that means," my son mumbled as he shook his head and walked away.

Have you ever felt that tug at your heart as you saw a person in need? I know you have felt that tug. Everyone feels that tug within themselves at various points in their life. You know why? Because we are all born with the breath of God within us. Believer or not, we've all been born with the breath of God. Some of us come into relationship with the Holy Spirit through our trust in Jesus, and others, sadly, don't. We all, however, are given life—the Spirit is the breath of life.

The goals of God's mission are twofold—salvation and justice. God longs for all humanity to experience peace with God, self, others, and the entire cosmos through the redemption provided by the death, burial, and resurrection of Jesus. God's express agency for delivering this peace is the church, that is, you and me. We are the agents that God is using to make God's appeal to this world. We are called, as the church and as guided by the Holy Spirit, to work toward providing wholeness for the world. We are called to "unbreak" the broken world. God desires a world unbroken and makes this real through the way the church lives out the virtues of Jesus as it discerns the way the Spirit is leading.

Chances are you are reading this book as a leader of leaders or as a disciple maker looking for ways to help people form spiritually. You could probably fill the margins of this page with dozens of names of people you are either intending to disciple or currently discipling (feel free to do so!). I can't say it any plainer than this: if you want to faithfully lead and disciple, you must not move without the presence and power of the Spirit. If so, you'll be like my friend and I that summer sitting in the boat in the middle of the lake waiting for the boat to move swiftly only to sit and wait. Gladhearted disciples realize the importance of catching the wind, the Holy Spirit, to lead them along the way. Gladhearted disciples long to stand in the heart of what Jesus is calling them to, and the only way they know where that place is located is to pray for the Holy Spirit's guidance and direction.

Part Five

⟡

THE GLADHEARTED DISCIPLE-MAKING LEADER

Chapter 10

The Gladhearted Disciple as Leader

I t isn't enough to make gladhearted disciples. As leaders of ministry initiatives, small groups, mission initiatives, congregations, Sunday school classes, and so on, we've got to seek not only to inspire, challenge, encourage, and equip disciples but also to make disciples who lead others toward being gladhearted disciples. Making followers is easy. Making disciples is a little harder. Making disciples who are leaders is the hardest of the three.

When was the last time you asked someone to lead? Responses may include, "I am happy to help but I do not want to lead" or "I am not a leader, I am just a helper" or even "I could never be a leader, I am just a volunteer." Have you ever heard these responses? Seeking disciples who are ready to take the next step toward becoming a leader can be difficult in and of itself. Finding people who have the skills, gifts, and talents to lead who actually want to lead is becoming harder all the time.

I've come to realize, through my own leadership trials, failures, and even triumphs, that when it comes to leading and recruiting and training and nurturing and sustaining leaders, the key issue is *who*, not the what, how, where, and why that inspire people toward accepting a position of leadership. Who you are as a person and as a leader has more impact on people than what you do, how you do it, and where you do it. The what, how, and where (and certainly why) matter greatly but only within the context of who a leader is becoming. Do the people you are recruiting to be leaders, to help you in your mission as a Christian and as a church, see the things you do or do they see who you are and who you are becoming?

A few weeks ago I was searching for a leader who would take the reins of a new group of young twenty-something couples who decided that the time was right for them to come together and commit to being a group—for a minimum of six weeks. I find that in my church's context many people who long to be in a group don't want to just jump right in and commit to a lifetime of being in a small group. Sometimes it works out that way but it is important to give a new group the chance to jump ship after six weeks. Not everyone is meant to be in a group forever. There are many reasons for this but mostly it has to do with trying on something to see if it works. While community is both organization and essence, not everyone is ready to commit to a long-term commitment with people they have never met or only met on several occasions. Anyway, I asked a couple to lead this new group. The response I got was simple and to the point: "Chris, I am not sure you want us to lead. Our life is a mess right now. We can barely lead ourselves. Our kids are a mess; our jobs are causing us a lot of stress." They continued, "We need a strong leader to lead us more than we need to be leaders for others. Maybe there is someone else you could find to lead our group?"

I said, "Well, I can understand that. I get it. At times I think I would have said my life was a mess too. No worries. Join the group, make some new friends, and grow in your faith. That's what I want most for you. Before I go, however, can you tell me what I should be looking for in a leader to lead your group? Can we take a few minutes to make a list?"

"Yes!" they both said emphatically.

So I got my iPad out, and we made the following list of foundational traits that they were looking for in a leader. I struck gold that day. If it were only that easy all the time!

1. **Every leader should know who he or she is.** Basically, what this young couple was saying is that whoever ends up leading the group needs to be someone who is real. Whoever leads the group should be someone who isn't trying to be anyone other than more of what God created them to be. Leaders who can reproduce other leaders are people who are not pretending and are able to be the real self that God designed them to be. So I ask you, who are you, really, and who are you becoming?

2. **Every leader should know what he or she wants to accomplish.** This couple thought, and I completely agree, that the leader should have a purpose and be guided by that purpose. Leaders should be principled people who are able to help those they are leading to move toward a common vision with focus and intentionality that

prevents them from wavering or grasping for a secret formula that will help them lead better. Instead, the ideal leader should be a faithful person, committed to the purpose of the church. In our case at Resurrection, we are looking for leaders who are working alongside the rest of us to build a Christian community where nonreligious and nominally religious people are becoming deeply committed Christians; seek leaders who will work toward that goal. Churches need leaders who will live into their mission and who know what they are trying to lead the group toward. So, I ask you, what are you trying to accomplish?

3 **Every leader should have a proper motivation.** This trait is extremely important. I run into "leaders" all the time who are leading for reasons other than what they should be. I ran into a guy the other day who admitted that he was leading a Sunday school class because he believes God has blessed him with the "right" theological views and other people need to know what they are. Being "right," friends, in not the kind of motivation that those who are following you are expecting from you. Who gets the glory? Whose mission is it anyway? A good leader leads out of a passion for a cause. When it comes to church leadership, leaders ought to lead for the sake of the world, that everyone might know who God is. So, I ask you, what is your motivation for leading?

4. **Every leader needs others to depend on.** I will admit it. One of the hardest things for me to do as a leader is to put my trust in someone else. I find it difficult, at times, to trust that others will execute at the level and with the quality that I desire to execute. The truth, if you must know, is that I struggle, as do many, with a desire to accumulate power. So I have to work really hard to deflect that desire and allow others to lead. I currently lead a team of twelve staff. Some of the staff I lead have been leading for many years. One guy has even been a senior pastor and a good one at that! Some of them have been around Resurrection for a decade longer than me. They are fully capable of leading, and some can lead circles around me. I have to train myself and retrain myself all the time to think bigger and depend on others. No one wants to follow a leader who controls everything and never gives others a chance to perform and lead. So, I ask you, whom are you depending on in order to lead the best way you could possibly lead?

5. **Every leader should be able to prioritize what is best for others.**
Along with depending on others, effective and healthy leaders will
be able to see the needs in others around them and do whatever
it takes to meet those needs. Leaders are able to take their focus
off themselves and make intelligent observations about the people
they are leading. Sometimes this is simple and sometimes this is
extremely difficult to identify. However, leaders who want the best
for the health of others are able to identify where others can grow
or even shine. A few weeks ago I noticed that one of the staff members on my team was sending me e-mails at 3:00 a.m. That's an
easy one. A harder one, however, was the woman on my team who
had it all together in front of everyone but would leave at lunch,
go out to her car, and weep over the stress in her life. In meetings,
on the phone, in the classes we taught, everything was going great.
No signs of difficulty. However, behind closed doors (car doors in
this instance), this woman struggled to keep moving through life.
Effective and healthy leaders are able to see the people they lead,
watch the progress or lack thereof, know them well enough to shape
and shepherd their life and prioritize others' lives over their own.
NOTE: Not to the extent that the leader becomes unhealthy, obvi-
ously. This should go without saying but, as leaders, we need to be
healthy in order to lead others. More on this in number 7 below.
So, I ask you, in what ways are you prioritizing the needs of those
you lead over your own needs?

6. **Every leader should learn from others.** A few years ago I was in a
mentee/mentoring relationship with a guy I knew who was in his
early seventies. This guy had been the CEO of major companies,
bought and sold companies, consulted with some of the greatest
leaders in the world, and sat in on meetings in some of the most
influential business mergers in history. I was fascinated with him.
He was everything I wanted to be: an effective leader who carried
himself with pride, and at every chance he got, praised others for
their greater role in all of his achievements. His humility was contagious. One day, when I walked into the restaurant where we always
met I noticed that my mentor was sitting with an older gentleman.
I watched for a bit as they laughed hard and just had a ball together.
I walked over to the booth where they were sitting and greeted my
mentor. He said, "Oh good. You are here. Finally! You are late. I am
glad you made it though. I want to introduce you to my mentor."

Then he introduced us. I stuck out my hand expecting a flimsy handshake from this guy who looked like he was in his late nineties (and he was!), and instead I got a firm and long handshake that came with a smile and an invitation to sit. My mentor who had been there and done it all had a mentor who had been there and done it all! My mentor went on to tell me how much he had learned from this guy, and if it weren't for this guy, he'd be a fraction of who he was that day. Effective and healthy leaders know where to go to get advice and learn from those who have gone before. Asking for help is not a sign of weakness; it is a sign of wisdom. So, I ask you, who are you learning from? Who is mentoring you?

7. **Every leader knows what to do to restore himself or herself.** I play golf with my two sons, who are eleven and nine. We have a blast! The golf is horrible but the time is amazing. I need to laugh. I need the sun. I need the time away. I need to leave my phone in my car. I need to just be dad. I've been leading long enough now that I know when I need to recreate myself. I know when I feel myself getting short with people. I know when I drive to the church and instead of feeling eagerness I feel sour. I know when I need a break. Sometimes I know only because the staff around me says, "You need a break." Or my wife says, "Why don't you go do something?" Every leader in history has needed to take a break. Sometimes it is nine holes of golf and sometimes it is several weeks off from leading. Restoring yourself is necessary if you wish to be more than a disciple maker and become a developer of other leaders. So, I ask you, in what ways are you refreshing yourself?

I am so glad that couple took the time to share the kind of leader they are looking for. Today, at Resurrection, we are looking for leaders who are real, on mission, motivated by the right things, able to depend on others, looking to help others before self, willing and seeking to learn from others, and intentionally taking time to restore themselves.

Chapter 11

Five Key Factors for the Mission Ahead

Gladhearted disciples are followers of Jesus who are generous people looking into the future through a lens of hope, accepting but not settling for what the world has become and yet determined to live in such a way that engages the world in Christ-centered mission, through the empowerment and guidance of the Holy Spirit, and with the purpose of recognizing the redemptive reign of God in every dimension of the Christian life.

The kingdom of God is what shapes the thinking, living, and being of the gladhearted disciples. Jesus's teachings on the kingdom of God are the guideposts to a gladhearted life. Gladhearted disciples, with all of their might, do whatever it takes to make earth look, feel, and be like heaven. Gladhearted disciples see their role on this earth as participants with God to restore the world toward its intended wholeness, and to make more gladhearted disciples. The kingdom of God provides the pattern for the gladhearted disciple's life.

There are, along with the other ideas in this book, several key factors when considering how the gladhearted disciple goes about his or her daily life engaging the world in Christ-centered mission as empowered by the Holy Spirit. These key factors help the gladhearted disciple stay focused for the mission at hand—cosmic restoration. The following five factors should be constantly remembered as we engage, embody, and express the mission of God for the sake of the world.

1. **Gladhearted disciples are prophets of a long road.** Prophets are people who convey God's word to a people. Prophets are called to proclaim and publicize God's words and God's work. In the Old Testament we know that God used prophets to show how God was going to interact with humans and history. Prophets gave their lives, willingly or not, to bring that foreseen reality to the people. Prophets help the people of the intended message to think on two major faults, namely self-centeredness and injustice. By *self-centeredness* I mean anything that keeps people from worshipping God first in their lives. By *injustice* I mean disregard for neighbor because of the selfishness in putting others' needs behind self or even completely out of mind. Gladhearted disciples are prophets. They recognize their role in proclaiming and publicizing God's words and work to a land full of self-centeredness and injustice. They point to the kingdom of God as God's intended plan for the world and do so by living, loving, and leading down a long, sometimes very long, road. Gladhearted disciples realize that the road for any prophet may be bumpy, stormy, dangerous, and long, and yet they don't waver. Relentlessly, even ruthlessly, gladhearted disciples announce the coming of the kingdom.

2. **Gladhearted disciples know their place, path, and purpose.**[1] *Practicing Witness: A Missional Vision of Christian Practices* by Benjamin Conner is a great little book full of extraordinary wisdom. One of the most helpful articulations of witness in Conner's book was his thoughtful expression of how ministry with adolescents involves helping them discover their place, path, and purpose. Their place is the social world, their path is how they integrate with their social world, and their purpose is their ongoing identity development within their place and down their path. I contend that this is also a great way for gladhearted disciples of any age to see their lives within their partnership in God's kingdom. Gladhearted disciples are aware of their social world, seek to intentionally integrate their own life with their social world, all the while being formed into the image and likeness of God for the sake of the world. As we engage the world with a Christ-centered mission, we are constantly aware of our place(s), path, and purpose.

3. **Gladhearted disciples keep Christian practices and their life so their life points to the kingdom of God.** No person's writing has

shaped my ministry thinking, doing, and being more than Lesslie Newbigin's. Newbigin was a British theologian, missionary, and author who wrote primarily about the church and mission. Newbigin's work declares that the church gets its purposes and priorities from the missionary heart of God. According to Newbigin, the church is sent into the world because God is a sending God with a mission to redeem the entire cosmos. Newbigin's work is arguably the largest contribution to the missional church movement today. Newbigin was useful to the church in many ways, one of which was in helping the church to think through three main elements of Christian practices. Christian practices are essentially symbols that make up a way of life and that point to the way things could be—on earth as it is in heaven, whole. Newbigin's three main elements are (1) signs, (2) instruments, and (3) foretaste.[2] Signs are the things Christians live out to show others the possibility beyond their current perspective or way of life. Signs give hope, now. Instruments are the things God uses to heal a broken world, and foretastes are the places which, because of the gladhearted disciples' way of life, provide a place where people can experience the coming joy and freedom now. In the end, these practices point to the kingdom. Gladhearted disciples seek to practice their faith through maintaining a healthy body, caring for creation, serving in the public affairs of society, practicing justice, and so on in order to point to the kingdom, giving people a sense of the reality of God and God's desired world for all of God's creation.

4. **Gladhearted disciples refuse to see people as an agenda.** One of the challenges that gladhearted disciples face and have to work tirelessly to overcome is the tendency to begin to see people as pawns in a chess game or pieces to a puzzle. I don't believe this tendency to be intended by any. No one, that I know of anyway, ever sets out to manipulate people like pieces to a board game. However, I do see from time to time within the church an inadvertent preoccupation with people as a means to an end. Gladhearted disciples work to overcome this depersonalization of the gospel by remembering that relationship becomes real when two people completely open themselves up to one another and respect one another's moral autonomy. Gladhearted disciples seek the integrity of the relationships by maintaining fellowship and community without asking the other(s) to surrender anything about themselves or those people

who make them who they are.[3] In the gladhearted leaders' line of work it is a regular occurrence for people to be different. This translates into people who are sometimes very difficult to be around and who require great amounts of grace, patience, forbearance, and love. We don't, we can't, ask these kinds of people to not be who they are because "love cannot violate the integrity of another. To do so cancels out love."[4] Gladhearted disciples work hard to make sure that the people they are engaging with the Christ-centered mission of God are not merely people on whom they impose their will and instead are people they invite into deep and personal relationships.

5. **Gladhearted disciples can see the kingdom on earth as it is in heaven.** Can you see it? Can you feel it? Can you taste it? Can you, a gladhearted disciple, truly live inside of the hope that Jesus promises within his kingdom teachings? Do you believe it? Do you truly believe that we are all beggars in the making? Meaning, do you believe as Saint Teresa did that "every time we pray The Lord's Prayer we are begging that God would use us to make it happen"?[5] Gladhearted disciples are beggars in the making. We are people who long for God to use us as people of the dust, the earth, to carry the reality of the kingdom. Gladhearted disciples, through the guidance and direction of the Holy Spirit, are accepting of the way things are in the world. They understand why the world is a broken place. However, the acceptance of this reality carries with it a greater reality that God is at work in the world to make all things new and that one day God will again dwell with God's people. This dwelling will be characterized by the peace of God, self, others, and the world, the very shalom in which the world was created. Gladhearted disciples might struggle with their gladness from time to time as they suffer with Jesus and mourn for the world. However, gladhearted disciples live with invincible trust that God, indeed, will reign. Gladhearted disciples are concerned about one thing—the kingdom of God, and the kingdom of God is anywhere God reigns.

I conclude this chapter with the passage of scripture I have often concluded other books with. May this portion of scripture be the way all gladhearted disciples look through the lens of hope for the world, I pray:

> How beautiful upon the mountains
> are the feet of a messenger

who proclaims peace,
who brings good news,
who proclaims salvation,
who says to Zion, "Your God rules!"

Listen! Your lookouts lift their voice;
    they sing out together!
    Right before their eyes they see the LORD returning to Zion.

Break into song together, you ruins of Jerusalem!
The LORD has comforted his people and has redeemed Jerusalem.
The LORD has bared his holy arm in view of all the nations;
all the ends of the earth have seen our God's victory. (Isa 52:7-10)

Chapter 12

Questions and Applications for the Gladhearted Leader

Questions for Reflection and Discussion

U se the following questions to guide your reflection on the contents of this book and to engage these on your teams, in your groups, or in your congregation.

Introduction

- Have you noticed a spirit of deconstruction in the leaders around you? In what ways are you positively or negatively responding to this spirit of deconstruction? Do you consider yourself a constructionist, a deconstructionist, or both? Why?

- What do you think about the author's definition of a gladhearted disciple? Do you find this to be a helpful definition for the production of disciples in your ministry context? Why or why not?

- What are your thoughts about discipleship being, in part, about finding contentment in suffering with Jesus?

- In what ways does hope orient and reorient your life? How might you describe what you so eagerly wait upon but do not occupy?

- In what ways have you experienced the bifurcation of mission and discipleship in your ministry contexts? How might you articulate the author's premise that discipleship is for mission?

- In what ways are you experiencing the reality of the Holy Spirit in your ministry context? In what ways do you find the work of the Holy Spirit and a faithful commitment to Christ-centered mission to be the same? Different?

- Describe what it means for gladhearted disciples to "live on mission." In what way would you describe the Beatitudes as blessings?

- In what ways is your congregation "bringing the redemptive reign of God in Christ into every dimension of life"?

Chapter One

- How do you define *apologetics*? What has been your experience with apologetics? Would you say that you are finding a need to redefine apologetics for the people in your ministry context? Why or why not?

- What do you think the author means by the phrase *missional instincts*? Do you agree or disagree with the author as to the idea of missional instincts and where they come from?

- How do you understand what it means to be created in the image of God? Why, according to the author, have we been created in the image of God?

- Using your own words, how would you define the natural, political, and moral image in which humans have been created?

- How does the author's statement, "It really isn't about how far skeptics are from God but rather just how closely they've been created to resemble God" make you feel? Do you agree or disagree with the author?

- What do you think the author means by the phrase *believability gap*?

- The author has listed a number of implications to what it means for gladhearted disciples to live out their missional instincts. What implications listed most deeply resonate with you? Are there any implications you experience that you would add to this list?

- What do you think the author means by living into a "new story"?

- According to the author, how and where do missional expressions emerge? In what ways do you think missional expressions benefit the ministry context you serve?

- What do you think the author means by the statement, "Love almost single-handedly measures the essence of beauty"? What else, in your opinion, measures the essence of beauty?

- What does the author suggest is the footing for a new apologetic? How is this a different starting place than with a more modern approach to apologetics?

- Do you find that fear regulates the way the people around you practice their faith? If so, in what ways?

- In what ways do the three aspects of mission—scripture, culture, and faith communities—work together to comprise the whole picture of God's mission?

- Name the three categories of missional expressions the author uses as a framework for everyday living. In what ways are you already living out these missional expressions?

Chapter Two

- When was the first time you heard the term *post-Christian*? How does this term make you feel?

- When it comes to Millennials, what do you think are the primary concerns when it comes to the validity of personal faith?

- In what ways can your congregation provide a larger framework of God for Millennials? How well do you think you are currently doing with this now?

- In what ways can gladhearted disciples create spaces for conversations, relationships, and inclusivity for Millennials?

- What are some of the "tough" questions that Millennials are expressing in your ministry context?

- How is the post-Christian culture we are living in a "blessing in disguise"?

- In what ways can gladhearted disciples take their faith into public spaces? How is your congregation already actively engaging in a public faith?

Chapter Three

- What does it mean to you to "search for the fullness in which we were created"? In what ways are you doing this on a daily basis?

- What do you think it means to see the world through a lens of grief? In what way are we "taking up residence with God" when we see the brokenness of this world through a lens of grief?

- What do you think it means to see the world through a lens of disgust? According to the author, what happens when we see the brokenness of this world through a lens of disgust?

- Describe a situation when you've seen another person act upon his or her disgust for this world. What was your reaction to his or her behavior?

- How would you describe what it means to accept the way the world is but expectantly wait for God's redemptive activity?

- In what ways are we able to "unbreak" the world?

Chapter Four

- How do you define the term *community*? What do you think the primary understanding of the term *community* is in your ministry context?

- Are you able to trust in the everyday good of others? Why or why not?

- What do you think it means to be attached to a story? In what ways is meaning important to people's understanding of community?

- What do you think it means for a community to see itself as being sent? Do the small groups in your ministry context typically see themselves as sent ones?

- What is it about human beings that makes them hunger for a deep sense and experience of community?

- According to the author, what are the essential ingredients of a true community? What else do you think could be added to the author's list of essential ingredients?

- When does a community cease to exist as a true community?

- In what ways do you think we can help disciples in our congregation offer themselves without expecting anything in return?

- In what ways does viewing God as love change the way we live? In what ways does it change the way we make disciples and develop leaders?

- What would it take for people in our groups to love, even when there is no promise of love returned?

- The author lists ten habits of healthy communities. What are the two or three habits listed that resonate most with you? What would you suggest to the author to add to the list?

Chapter Five

- In what ways would you describe the phrase *Christian perfection*?

- What do you think is required in life to live "fully human" as Jesus did?

- What is meant by social holiness?

- Do you think it is possible for a person to reach a state in which they do not willfully sin? What do you think it takes to reach this state?

- Why do humans exist? In what ways is love the central truth of the gospel?

- Do you think there is a difference between being made perfect and to be making perfect? How would you describe the difference?

- What is it, according to the author, that takes missional instincts and turns them into missional expressions?

- Describe several of the key metrics gladhearted disciples should use to measure their culture of disciple making.

- What do you think it means to "Let your soul be filled with so entire a love to him, that you may love nothing but for his sake"?[1]

Chapter Six

- When you think of the creation narratives in Genesis 1–2, what is your first thought?

- In what ways would you describe the way in which the four relationships interact with one another?

- How would you describe God's intended desire for wholeness? In what ways can you help make gladhearted disciples who see this as a priority for life?

- What makes it possible for peace with God, self, others, and the entire world not only plausible but promised?

- What is the speed at which peace and justice can be generated and formed? What are you doing in your current ministry context to make peace and justice real?

- In what ways are you currently educating your congregation to engage in efforts of peace and justice?

- According to the author, what is the force God is using to reconcile the world?

Chapter Seven

- Describe how the phrases "do you remember when" and "let me tell you a story" are different.

- How do the stories we share with others make meaning and give our lives direction?

- How is story currency for connection and community?

- In what ways can your congregation create shared narratives and be intentional about the experiences they create?

- What is your congregation's top three ways of inviting people to church?

- In what ways are you helping those you invite to participate in the story of your congregation? Would you say that those you invite appreciate your intentionality?

- How would you describe the difference between participation and contribution? In what ways are you helping people in your ministry context see themselves as contributors?

- How important do you think it is to evoke the imagination of people within your ministry context? In what ways are you currently painting a living rendering of what it looks like for heaven and earth to collide?

- Describe how you are currently trying to tell a larger, more dramatic, and more intense story than the people in your ministry context are currently living.

Chapter Eight

- What is it about your favorite prayer that makes it your favorite? In what ways do you find that prayer helps you in your pursuit toward Christian perfection?

- How does the fact that Jesus lived for the glory of God change the way you live? What is it about the first part of the prayer of Jesus (John 17:1-5) that resonates with you the most?

- In John 17:6-19 Jesus prays for his disciples. He prays that his disciples will be protected from the evil one as they live. In what ways does this particular part of Jesus's prayer inspire you?

- Finally, in John 17:20-26 Jesus prays directly for you and me— for all disciples. Jesus prays also for the sake of the world. In what ways are you committed to praying for the world?

- Does your faith community have a purpose or mission statement? If so, can you write it? If you were to place the phrase, "for the sake of the world" at the end of the statement, how would it enhance or change your statement?

- The author lists six attributes of kingdom living. What most resonates with you from this list? In what ways do these attributes shape the way you live, love, and lead?

- How would you describe the reason and role of the church? In what way does your congregation live out what it means to be the church? In what ways can you become more effective in your intentions to live, love, and lead for the sake of the world?

Chapter Nine

- According to the author, what is the key to movement in the Christian life? Describe what life with and without the Holy Spirit is like.

- In what ways is the Holy Spirit the core of the church's existence and sustenance?

- How does God choose to fulfill God's mission? What does it mean that the church is the agency of deliverance and salvation?

- According to the author, what is it that a generous community finds its true identity?

- In what ways does your faithfulness to the ministry of the Holy Spirit help your leadership?

- Why is it important for gladhearted disciples to live in the presence and power of the Holy Spirit?

- Take a moment and write down the names of five people whom you are discipling. What is it about each person that makes discipling them unique?

- Do you pray for the presence and power of the Holy Spirit? Take a moment right now and either write or say a prayer explicitly seeking the guidance of the Holy Spirit.

Chapter Ten

- When you ask a person in your congregation to join you in leading others, what is the most common response you hear?

- How does who you are as a person most directly influence your ability to recruit, train, inspire, and equip leaders?

- Why is it important or even imperative to be real as a leader?

- Why is it critical for leaders to set goals for the people they are leading?

- What would you say is your motivation as a leader? What do you think is the primary motivation of others who lead with you?

- Describe how the ability to trust and depend on others is crucial to a leader's character.

- How effective are you at prioritizing what is better for those you lead rather than what is best for you?

- Do you believe it is important for you as a leader to learn from others? If yes, who are you learning from and why?

- What types of activities do you engage in as a leader that restore or refresh you?

Chapter Eleven

- After being introduced to the definition of a gladhearted disciple in the introduction and then reading it again in chapter 11, how do you feel about it? Does the definition work for you to help you have a framework for discipleship? Why or why not?

- In what ways does the kingdom of God give us a pattern for how to live as participants in God's mission to restore the world toward its intended wholeness?

- Have you ever thought of yourself as a prophet? In what ways do we all as gladhearted disciples serve our communities as prophets?

- How well do you know your ministry context? How often do you take time to exegete your context?

- In what ways are Christian practices a foretaste of the kingdom of God?

- How do you deal with difficult people? Do you ever find yourself trying to avoid them? How might you become more intentional with discipling difficult people?

- The author suggests that gladhearted disciples are beggars in the making. Keeping the Lord's Prayer in mind, in what ways are each of us beggars?

Chapter Twelve

- How do you think the people in your congregation will react to your desired changes?

- How well do you know your ministry context? In what ways will you seek to discover the most accurate context you can before setting out on the change journey?

- How quickly do you think you'll be able to form a team? What makes the team diverse, energetic, and purposeful?

- In what ways will shifting the power to others be difficult for you? What checks and balances can you put around you to help you with this?

- What metrics will you use to evaluate how effective your change process is?

- In what ways can you instill a sense of urgency but keep from allowing panic to set in?

- How clearly can you articulate the "why" behind your vision? Have you attempted to share your vision with others? How well do they receive it? Are there others you have shared it with able to articulate the vision as well as or better than you?

- In what ways are you getting yourself and the team ready for the long road ahead?

Making Change Happen

"Change is inevitable, except from a vending machine." Humorous but true words reportedly once quipped by Robert C. Gallagher, a businessman and former director of the storied Green Bay Packers football franchise. Gallagher's words might make us chuckle but the process of change and the inevitability of it can lead to great amounts of frustration, irritation, and so on.

It is very likely that in order to integrate some of the ideas in this book into your daily ministry context, you'll need to be ready to embrace the frustrations and irritations that come with advancing change. As you know, some people love change. It is usually the people creating it, however, who love it. Change is difficult for many, and as the person responsible for change in your context you'll need a well-thought-out plan to navigate all that comes with wanted and unwanted change.

I'll offer a ten-step change process that I have used several times throughout my years in ministry. This process has been tweaked over the years as I have learned from many failures and triumphs. Like any framework or process, it will be imperative for you to contextualize it to most accurately and effectively meet your needs for change as you build a culture of gladhearted disciple making.

Step One: Know your ministry context

Few of the leaders I have consulted with over the years have taken the time to truly know their ministry context. Of course, this is something we should be doing all the time but, unfortunately, few do. As the ministry changes (grows, shrinks, innovates, dies, etc.) it is unescapably altered and transformed into something dissimilar to what you've ever known. When was the last time you determined the realities and confirmed the presumptions of your particular ministry? In order to effectively make change and sustain change, you'll need to be an expert in every facet of your ministry.

Step Two: Determine exactly why you are changing and exactly what it is you are trying to accomplish with the change

Once you've established a firm and accurate understanding of your ministry context you'll need to determine just what it is you are changing. Are you merely changing programs or are you trying to change a culture? Are you seeking to develop a new model or are you simply tweaking an already established model? Once you determine just what it is you are trying to change, in the end, what will the result of this change be? I recommend holding off on any change process until you can clearly articulate (verbally and in writing) what the outcomes of the change will be.

Step Three: Start talking about it as a mere idea and watch and listen

In the past, as I implemented various amounts of change in various ministry settings, I found it very helpful to begin leaking out some of my ideas for change. Typically, I do this by asking key influencers questions such as, "What if we were to change the way we approach making disciples?

How might that impact our overall ministry?" Questions disarm people. Statements can often put people on the defensive. Sharing some questions with a few not only gives you the chance to test your ideas, it gives you somewhat of an understanding of the opposition you may face. As you share your ideas be sure to watch and listen well. Body language, returned questions, and responses might tell you all you need to know about how difficult the change process might be.

Step Four: Build a diverse, energetic, purposeful team

The only way to make effective and lasting change is to work with a team. You will need a team of diverse people to share this process of change with. You will need people who are not like you. You will need people who are smarter than you. You will need people who are more experienced than you. You will need people who are willing to push back on your ideas and refine them while doing so. You will need people who have the energy to lead through the frustrations and irritations of people and not quit when it gets tough. You will need a team of people who live with purpose and live on mission. In the end, you will need a team of people who are willing to do whatever it takes to engage the change process with humility, meaning, and passion. NOTE: In some ministry contexts I discovered the need for change and I was able to see and articulate what the outcomes of change would be. However, I didn't have the right team in place. Sometimes, before you can implement change at any level, you need to spend time developing a team.

Step Five: Design a working ministry model

People need for you to be practical. The people on your team and the people who will be experiencing the change and living into the new culture will need for you to articulate a new model. The common question at this stage from your team and from others is, "Once we make the changes, what will the new culture look like?" If you are going to birth the change process and build a team to help you accomplish your vision, you must be able to articulate, write, sketch, and so on the framework for making disciples.

Step Six: Set team goals and determine tasks, as a team

Once your draft selections have been made and you've assembled the team to help you, and you've determined a working framework or model, begin developing the goals and assigning the necessary tasks to accomplish the vision. Goals and tasks will be very contextual and specific. Goals and tasks at this stage help people on the team know not only what they are doing and how to do it but in what ways their particular role is making a significant contribution.

Step Seven: Develop partnerships with other departments/ministry areas

You'll need allies to help you make effective and lasting change. In what other areas of the church can you begin to recruit and train allies that get what you are trying to accomplish? Perhaps a few people from children's or worship or missions can help you by articulating the need for change and the positive outcomes as a result of the change? It is powerful for a person (especially a naysayer) to hear from another congregant or staff person outside of your scope of responsibility that the changes being made are going to make a big change in the overall ability of the church to make disciples.

Step Eight: Shift the power to others on the team

This step is hard for so many leaders. Unfortunately, this step is where so many people who set out with good intentions for change get caught up. This step is where leaders can get so stuck that the change project shuts down. In order to fully maximize the team members and their skills and gifts for the sake of change and a new vision, you may be required to shift the power or leadership reins to others. If you are a collaborative, missional leader this will not be a problem for you. If you are a lone-ranger type leader, this will be a big struggle for you. You may have to give up the right to be right and let others lead even where you don't think it is best. Clearly, you need to protect the vision. It is how you choose to protect the vision that is key.

Step Nine: Lead by providing encouragement, tools, and resources

One of the most important and helpful ways you can help your team is to consistently provide them with tools and resources to get their job done. Whether paid or volunteer, the team will need constant coaching, encouragement, inspiration, and tools to accomplish the tasks the team set out to accomplish. This is what leaders do. Leaders find meaningful ways to help their teams get better. You'll need to determine what your team and the individuals on your team need to see the change become reality.

Step Ten: Make it happen, measure results, and evaluate and modify

As you begin to implement the necessary changes to accomplish the shared vision of the team, you'll need measuring devices that help you know how to evaluate the changes and modify the new model for maximum effectiveness. Sometimes the measurements or metrics are based on numbers. Sometimes they are based on the stories you are hearing. Sometimes numbers and stories will help you evaluate and modify. Determining the necessary metrics will be helpful for knowing how you are doing.

Along with the ten steps above, I have found it very helpful to keep the following in play throughout the entire change process.

1. **Pray.** This will be key as you discern where the Holy Spirit is leading and guiding.

2. **Dream.** Never stop dreaming and letting your team dream about the future. Dreaming helps everyone feel as though there is always more that can be done and more that they can do.

3. **Have Urgency.** Without creating a sense of panic or instilling fear, it will be important to keep the change process moving by sharing how important the change is and how it will help live into the mission of God.

4. **Focus.** Sometimes teams trying to make change happen can spend the bulk of their time talking about how bad the past model or

former leader or whatever is. Focus your team on the new thing, not the old.

5. **Learn.** Clearly to stop learning through this process would be foolish. Learn as much as you can from as many as you can for as many as you can.

6. **Ask Why.** Don't ever lose the "why" behind what you are doing. Once you forget the why, the change process will be on a trajectory toward complete failure. Reminding yourself and the team of the "why" behind what you are doing is critical to the success of the change process.

Finally, it is important to remember that change takes time. You may feel urgency is good—as long as it doesn't manufacture a timeframe for seeing change become a reality that is not possible. You must be willing to walk the long road and keep in mind that change takes time. Don't rush it. Be patient. You will want to hurry it along, but pushing too hard too fast can lead to disaster. Keep the big picture in mind but keep the small things in front of you. Think big, act small. I recommend that the team implementing change speak in terms of 8-10 degree shifts. Need to make a 180-degree shift? That means that your actions, decisions, steps, and so on that are a mere 8-10 degrees can take months or even years to accomplish. Successful change agents live into the art of the long view.

Notes

Introduction

1. This list is taken from *Jesus is Lord: The Common Cry of a Kingdom Citizen*, youth edition by Chris Folmsbee and Ben Simpson © 2013 by Beacon Hill Press of Kansas City, Kansas City, MO. Used by permission of Publisher. All rights reserved. Visit our website at www.beaconhillbooks.com to purchase this title.

1. A New Apologetic for a Post-Christian World

1. Kenneth Collins, *The Theology of John Wesley: Holy Love and the Shape of Grace* (Nashville: Abingdon Press, 2007), 52.

2. Ibid.

3. In my book *Story, Signs and Sacred Rhythms* (Grand Rapids: Zondervan, 2010), I define the gospel as the story of God's will, way, and work of providing salvation and justice through the gift of his Son, Jesus Christ, for all of humanity. Faithful people understand that the gospel is (1) the entire narrative of God, (2) both salvation *and* justice, and (3) open for all of humanity to embrace and confess.

4. Mildred Wynkoop, *A Theology of Love* (Kansas City, MO: Beacon Hill Press, 1972), title page.

5. 1 Pet 3:15.

6. Joseph Gremillion, *The Gospel of Peace and Justice* (Maryknoll, NY: Orbis Books, 1976), ix.

4. The Organization and Essence of Community

1. Mildred Wynkoop, *A Theology of Love* (Kansas City, MO: Beacon Hill Press, 1972), 31.

2. John Wesley, "The Case of Reason Impartially Considered," *The Works of John Wesley*, ed. Albert C. Outler (Nashville: Abingdon Press, 1985), 2:598.

5. Revisiting Christian Perfection

1. Steven W. Manskar, *A Perfect Love: Understanding Wesley's "A Plain Account of Christian Perfection"* (Nashville: Discipleship Resources, 2002), 6.

2. Mildred Wynkoop, *A Theology of Love* (Kansas City, MO: Beacon Hill Press, 1972).

3. Eugene Peterson, *The Jesus Way: A Conversation on the Ways That Jesus Is the Way* (Grand Rapids: William B. Eerdmans, 2007), 37.

4. John Wesley, "The Circumcision of the Heart," *The Works of John Wesley*, ed. Albert C. Outler (Nashville: Abingdon Press, 1984), 1:413.

7. Creating "Do You Remember When?" Stories

1. Daniel Taylor, *Tell Me a Story* (St. Paul, MN: Bog Walk Press, 2001), 6.

2. Ibid.

3. Ibid., 3.

4. Ibid., 1.

8. Understanding the Reason and Role of the Church

1. Scot McKnight, *The Jesus Creed: Loving God, Loving Others* (Brewster, MA: Paraclete Press, 2004), 70.

2. Robert H. Ennis, "The Super-Streamlined Conception of Critical Thinking," The Critical Thinking Co., June 20, 2002, http://www.criticalthinking.com/articles/critical-thinking -definition.

3. Barry Beyer, quoted in "Evaluating Resources," Isothermal Community College, http:// www.isothermal.edu/library/evalinfo.htm.

4. Benedict of Nursia, *The Rule of Saint Benedict,* trans. Anthony C. Meisel and M. L. del Mastro (New York: Bantam Doubleday Dell Publishing, 1975), 89.

5. George G. Hunter III, *The Celtic Way of Evangelism: How Christianity Can Reach the West . . . Again,* rev. ed. (Nashville: Abingdon Press, 2010), 41.

9. Catching the Wind

1. Craig Van Gelder, *The Ministry of the Missional Church: A Community Led by the Spirit* (Grand Rapids, MI: Baker Books, 2007).

2. Jürgen Moltmann, "The Church in the Power of the Spirit," in *The Holy Spirit in the World Today*, ed. Jane Williams (London: Alpha International, 2001), 23.

3. Teresa of Avila, "Christ Has No Body," found at *Journey with Jesus* (webzine), http:// www.journeywithjesus.net/PoemsAndPrayers/Teresa_Of_Avila_Christ_Has_No_Body.shtml.

11. Five Key Factors for the Mission Ahead

1. Benjamin Conner, *Practicing Witness: A Missional Vision of Christian Practices* (Grand Rapids: Wm. B. Eerdmans, 2011).

2. Lesslie Newbigin, *A Word in Season: Perspectives on Christian World Missions* (Grand Rapids: Wm. B. Eerdmans, 1994).

3. Mildred Wynkoop, *A Theology of Love* (Kansas City, MO: Beacon Hill Press, 1972), 169.

4. Ibid.

5. St. Teresa of Avila, *The Way of Perfection* (Rockford, IL: Tan Books and Publishers, 1997), 191.

12. Questions and Applications for the Gladhearted Leader

1. John Wesley, "The Circumcision of the Heart," *The Works of John Wesley*, ed. Albert C. Outler (Nashville: Abingdon Press, 1984), 1:413.